Once a Month Cooking

Jody Allen was made redundant in 2011 while on maternity leave and pregnant with her second child, born 12 months after the first baby. She started her website, Stay at Home Mum, to share her money-saving experiences while her family lived on one wage and it has since become Australia's biggest mothers' network. Jody now connects with hundreds of thousands of women and has created a successful business. She started shopping, cooking and freezing in bulk to save time and money while still giving her family delicious, nutritious meals. Jody lives in Gympie, Queensland, with her husband and two boys.

stayathomemum.com.au

Once a Month Cooking

Jody Allen

MICHAEL JOSEPH
an imprint of
PENGUIN BOOKS

MICHAEL JOSEPH

Published by the Penguin Group
Penguin Group (Australia)
707 Collins Street, Melbourne, Victoria 3008, Australia
(a division of Penguin Australia Pty Ltd)
Penguin Group (USA) Inc.
375 Hudson Street, New York, New York 10014, USA
Penguin Group (Canada)
90 Eglinton Avenue East, Suite 700, Toronto, Canada ON M4P 2Y3
(a division of Penguin Canada Books Inc.)
Penguin Books Ltd
80 Strand, London WC2R 0RL England
Penguin Ireland
25 St Stephen's Green, Dublin 2, Ireland
(a division of Penguin Books Ltd)
Penguin Books India Pvt Ltd
11 Community Centre, Panchsheel Park, New Delhi 110 017, India
Penguin Group (NZ)
67 Apollo Drive, Rosedale, Auckland 0632, New Zealand
(a division of Penguin New Zealand Pty Ltd)
Penguin Books (South Africa) (Pty) Ltd
Rosebank Office Park, Block D, 181 Jan Smuts Avenue, Parktown North, Johannesburg 2196, South Africa
Penguin (Beijing) Ltd
7F, Tower B, Jiaming Center, 27 East Third Ring Road North, Chaoyang District, Beijing 100020, China
Penguin Books Ltd, Registered Offices: 80 Strand, London WC2R 0RL, England

First published by Penguin Group (Australia), 2014

1 3 5 7 9 10 8 6 4

Text copyright © Jody Allen, 2014
Photography copyright © Paul Harris, 2014

The moral right of the author has been asserted

Cover design by Laura Thomas © Penguin Group (Australia)
Text design by Pauline Haas © Penguin Group (Australia)
Photography by Paul Harris
Typeset in Bauer Bodini by Pauline Haas
Printed and bound in China by 1010 Printing International Ltd

National Library of Australia

Cataloguing-in-Publication data:
Allen, Jody, author
Once a Month Cooking / Jody Allen
ISBN: 9780143799689
1. Make-ahead cooking. 2. Cooking
3. Quantity cooking. 4. Home economics

641.555

To my beautiful husband, Brendan – my best friend, confidant, whipping boy and lover. Without his love, support and patience, there is no way this book would ever have been done. Thanks, Brenny – you're brilliant and I appreciate you so much! And to my two rambunctious sons, it is my sincerest hope that you grow up to be just like your father.

Contents

Introduction

If the thought of cooking a month's worth of meals in one day freaks you out, don't panic! This book will give you all the information you need to cook, freeze and serve a huge variety of dishes, so that you don't waste time, money or food. (It is estimated that Australians waste about nine million dollars worth of food per week! To me that is just not acceptable.) It will also mean that you're never more than a few minutes from having a meal on the table.

When I was pregnant with my second child, I knew I would be time-poor at night during 'arsenic hour' (actually about 4 p.m. until 10 p.m. at my place). Hubby would get home from work tired and cranky, my toddler needed his bath and everyone was hungry and wanted dinner on the table. I wanted to feed my family something healthy, quick and filling, but because I was so tired, quite often I would resort to pre-packaged foods or takeaway. Being on one wage, it was costing us a fortune. Money was going down the drain, and it wasn't good for our health either.

I can't take credit for coming up with the concept of Once a Month Cooking, but when I discovered it I was enticed by how it seemed to be a perfect fit for my lifestyle. However, most of the books and websites about freezer cooking that I found were US-focused and had totally different ingredients and measurements to what I was used to. It was then I came up with the idea of adapting the concept for an Australian audience. I wanted to make meals that my family would eat, find ways to get more vegetables into their diet, buy in bulk to save money and most importantly, save myself time during the busiest part of the day.

My next-door neighbour Corinne was pregnant at the same time and we decided to each do a huge cook and exchange half the meals. That way we'd both have a broader range of dishes in our freezers. We ended up with about 12 delicious choices of meals each for when the new babies came. It was a great success. When the first month's dishes were nearly finished, I had another go. Second time around was much easier as I knew what I was doing.

Usually all I have to do with a frozen meal is reheat it, and maybe add some steamed vegetables, top with pastry or cook some noodles. That's it; the meal is done. Sometimes there isn't even that much work, and, best of all, my children can often help out too because the preparation is so simple. I'm also teaching them time management and reinforcing the importance of home-cooked meals and that, to me, is a lesson money can't buy.

These days I can pretty much have a month's worth of food cooked in about five hours. Of course now that my kids are a bit older and I have a bit more time, we don't eat from the freezer every night, so I usually save the frozen meals for the evenings I don't feel like cooking and would be tempted to buy takeaway.

Hubby, by the way, loves my freezer cooking. He became sick of sandwiches for lunch and often felt like something warm to take to work in the colder months. Now he just goes to the freezer and chooses a delicious, nutritious meal. Usually I freeze meal portions for the whole family, but have adapted my technique so that there are a few single serves as well, because he's not the only one who likes a warm lunch on a cold day. Hubby used to spend about 12 dollars per day on lunch, but not anymore! He reckons a home-cooked lunch is so much tastier, with the added benefit of saving us a fortune!

That's the beauty of Once a Month Cooking – you cook the meals your family loves according to your lifestyle. If you are vegetarians who love a bit of extra chilli, or big meat eaters who don't fancy a lot of rice with your curry, you can adapt the recipes to suit your family's needs and desired portion sizes.

The purpose of this book is to help you do this in your own home – to plan, cook, freeze and serve a whole range of meals for your family – and to give you some tips and tricks from my own experiences that can save you even more time.

There is no reason you have to be a slave to the kitchen any longer!

How You Do It

Getting Started

WHAT IS ONCE A MONTH COOKING?

Do you dread that time of day when you have to decide on, prepare and cook dinner for your family? Do you stand in front of your pantry and fridge thinking 'What on earth are we going to eat tonight?' or 'What can I put in the kids' lunch boxes today?' only to decide it's all too hard and settle on something quick, simple and probably cooked by somebody else and put into a box for convenient consumption? Wouldn't you love to have a freezer full of home-cooked, nutritious, custom-made meals simply waiting for you to pull out and spend mere minutes preparing for your family? Just think what you could do with all that free time!

Once a Month Cooking is the ultimate pre-prepared meal technique. It is a method of cooking large batches of your normal family meals and filling your freezer with family-sized serves to make cooking easier. This concept is also known as Freezer Cooking or Investment Cooking.

The basic principle behind Once a Month Cooking is that you cook all your main dishes for a month in one day, freeze them, and then have an assortment of homemade meals to prepare quickly when you need to. These meals should only need minimal preparation when they are defrosted, such as adding vegetables, cooking pasta, covering with pastry or adding fresh herbs. You can also make snacks, biscuits and other bulk recipes for the kids to take for lunch or to have when they get home from school. Once a Month Cooking also allows you to pre-prepare desserts and cakes, so entertaining is easy.

WHAT ARE THE BENEFITS OF ONCE A MONTH COOKING?

The benefits of Once a Month Cooking outweigh the initial work involved in that it not only gives you back precious time but also saves you money. You buy in bulk, which results in a lower price per serving, and always having a meal on hand means you won't be turning to costly takeaways. Home-cooked meals are also generally much healthier than takeaway or pre-packaged options. You will have no wastage of food in your house by doing Once a Month Cooking, and it can even save you in electricity costs as you are not turning appliances on and off every evening cooking a full family dinner.

It can alleviate the stress of inviting guests over when you know you have something suitable just waiting to be defrosted. And, best of all, with Once a Month Cooking, you've not only whipped up 30 meals, but you've also created a month's worth of freedom from the kitchen (well, mostly!). Take the kids for a walk, have a bubble bath or read an extra chapter in your book – you've earned it!

A bit of time and money invested over a weekend really can make a huge difference to your budget, your health and your family's quality time together.

IS ONCE A MONTH COOKING A LOT OF WORK?

It is a lot of work ... but only for two days of the month! You'll have a day to do your shopping and another to do your cooking, and that's pretty much it. It's so much faster than cooking from scratch every night. What's more, practice makes perfect. When I started Once a Month Cooking it would take me all day, now I can have it down pat in about five hours.

WHAT IF I DON'T LIKE THE THOUGHT OF EATING FROZEN FOOD?

Freezer cooking is terrific for busy mums, but it isn't for everyone. If you love a fresh leafy salad on its own every night, then of course it won't be for you. But you can enjoy the best of both worlds. Make a fresh leafy salad and choose recipes you do like that are freezable.

Most people who haven't enjoyed frozen food in the past have had a bad experience with food that is not suitable for freezing or that was not frozen correctly or in the right packaging. This of course alters the taste, texture and appeal of the food. This book only focuses on meals and sweets that rock in the freezer.

WHAT IF MY FAMILY DON'T LIKE THE RECIPES?

To make Once a Month Cooking work for your family you have to cook to their tastes. Find the recipes that you know your family will love. This book contains simple, easy to make meals. Nothing fancy. They have all been tried and tested in my own kitchen, and eaten by my family on a regular basis, so I know what works.

Apart from the terrific recipes in this book, we have a huge freezer cooking section on the Stay at Home Mum website (stayathomemum.com.au) which is added to regularly, so you can keep discovering new dishes to feed your family.

My tip would be to stick to recipes your family love, and then try one serving of something new to see if they like it. If they do, make a huge batch. But there is nothing worse than cooking a huge batch of food your family won't eat!

DO I NEED A HUGE FREEZER?

Not at all. You can do Once a Week Cooking, or just cook a double batch of a recipe to have an extra meal on hand. Always cook to your family's needs and requirements, and that includes the size of your freezer.

When I started Once a Month Cooking I only had the small freezer over my fridge. But I loved it so much that I did invest in a large upright freezer. It has been the best investment ever.

IS FROZEN FOOD SAFE?

Freezing food is a great way to preserve its flavours. It is entirely safe to freeze most foods (see page 21 for the few exceptions). The key is making sure you thaw the dish correctly. I give you detailed thawing instructions for each recipe. There's more on thawing on page 22.

Planning

It's all in the planning! Proper planning and preparation are the key things that will allow you to manage everything that needs to go into the process of Once a Month Cooking. The more time you spend in the planning, the quicker and smoother the process, making for a more enjoyable experience! There's nothing worse than getting all excited and ready to cook, only to find out you picked a day full of distractions or didn't buy enough of an essential ingredient.

You have to plan how you're going to manage your time, plan each meal before even going shopping, organise your shopping list and determine your budget. The whole process will be much easier if you take a few hours to figure out a game plan before jumping onto the court.

There are four major steps that go into the process before you even start to cook. These are:

* Choose a cooking day
* Plan the monthly menu
* Make a shopping list and set a budget
* Get your kitchen organised

Each one of these steps is just as important as another, and together they are what will make your Once a Month Cooking session a success!

CHOOSE A COOKING DAY

Before you plan your meals or lift a finger to shop or cook, you need to choose the day when it is all going to take place. Choose your day carefully — it should be one with minimal distractions and commitments. A weekend day is usually the most effective, particularly if you have young children. You can get your partner to watch the kids while you cook, especially if you prefer to cook on your own without interruption from others. Alternatively, get a family member or friend to watch the kids and do your Once a Month Cooking with your partner. If you have school-age children perhaps a school day will work better for you, or if you want to get the whole family involved, save it for the weekend.

Another option is to cook with a friend. There are loads of advantages to cooking with someone else, including:

Share Recipes
You can have more of a choice in recipes when someone else is doing half of the work. You might even find a new family favourite!

Share the Workload
One person can be chopping and dicing whilst the other is stirring and packing. It really isn't any harder to cook for two families than it is to cook for one.

Share the Equipment
This is a big advantage. Not everyone has all the equipment that will make cooking easier, so pool your resources.

Share the Cost
Bulk deals will always save you money! Shop around and swap knowledge of good deals so you pay as little for the ingredients as you possibly can.

The idea is to utilise the entire day, but if you feel a bit overwhelmed at this prospect, consider cooking over two days, or in the evening. You will quickly find out what works best for you, your kitchen and your family. It's also good to plan a day when you have run down your freezer stocks so you have plenty of storage space. This also lets you see just exactly what you have left to use in your freezer before you start making your menu plan.

PLAN THE MONTHLY MENU

This step is very important. The goal is to decide which meals you will eat for each day of the month, keeping in mind your family's preferences, dietary needs, events and occasions throughout the month – all while providing healthy meals with a bit of variety.

Tip from a SAHM

I meal plan so that I use the same meat to make as many dishes as I can. *SUE JONES*

You need to decide how you are going to keep track of each individual meal, its ingredients and how many times you will eat it during the month. For example, you may make two or three batches of Bolognaise Sauce (page 68), as it's a family favourite and an easy choice for a weeknight when everyone is coming and going with sports and after-school classes.

When you are first starting Once a Month Cooking, you want to stick to basic recipes that you do well. Now's not the time to be experimenting with a recipe you haven't tried before. Save the experimenting for a night you do decide to cook from scratch. After all, you don't want to make a huge batch then nobody eats it!

Plan also to get as many vegetables as possible into your cooking. Not only is it healthy, it's a great way to 'bulk up' meals inexpensively and make your dollars go even further.

One method that works is starting a spreadsheet on your computer. You can decide as a family what meals you would like to have during the month and allocate them to certain days. You could also use this spreadsheet to keep track of after-school activities and upcoming engagements. Be sure to save your spreadsheet as a template for next month's cooking.

When you choose your meals, keep in mind the following tips:

* Get the family involved. Ask everyone to tell you or write down their favourite meals to include on the menu plan.

* Check out what is on special on your shopping day. One of the aims of Once a Month Cooking is to save money. Plan your meals around ingredients you can get cheaply.

* Plan ahead for nights out, trips away or guests for dinner. Prepare an extra special meal if you are hosting a dinner party, or if you are planning on being away on holiday, don't cook for the full month.

* Allocate a day or two for new recipes. Try something new on these days (these will be cooked from scratch).

It's a great idea to stick your list on the front of your freezer to keep track of what's on hand.

Plan for Variety

One thing that you don't want to do (unless you want a mutiny on your hands) is schedule the same type of meal for several days in a row. If you have three or four recipes that use basically the same ingredients, split them up so that you only eat each one once or twice a week.

Plan meals according to the season too; you don't want too many hot slow cooker meals or soups in summer, and fruit and vegetables are much nicer – and cheaper – when in season. Check out our table of seasonal fruit and vegetables on the website to maximise your nutrition and minimise your spending!

Sometimes it works to just have a list of what you have in the freezer without scheduling them into days. That way you can cater to your family's cravings on the day and let them pick what they feel like. It's also great for when you have a change of plans for dinner, such as an unexpected vegetarian guest or kids going out to friends and you've got half your usual brood to feed. Just make sure you allow enough time for defrosting.

Getting your family interested and involved in the planning stages really does make a big difference. Much like getting the kids into the kitchen to help prepare a meal, allowing them to contribute in the selection and planning of the menu makes them feel like they've had a say and they are more likely to help out – or leave you to it, whichever you prefer!

MAKE A SHOPPING LIST AND SET A BUDGET

Once you have your meals planned out for the month, it's time for the all-important master shopping list. You need to break down each recipe into ingredients (right down to the last garlic clove) and check your pantry, fridge and freezer for what you already have on hand. This process can take a bit of time so make sure you have time to correctly note down all the required ingredients for the portions you wish to make. Start by going through each recipe one by one. With the first recipe, list the ingredients and the quantities, and for each of the following recipes add to the quantities already listed.

Using a spreadsheet program on your computer can be helpful in more ways than one. It keeps a record of your master list should you wish to make certain recipes again, and is a lot more organised than the traditional paper and pen approach. You will find you will need to adjust quantities and add ingredients to certain sections and this is so much cleaner and quicker with a spreadsheet. Family members can add to it and when you print it off to go shopping, you don't have a huge mess of different handwriting to decipher.

Our example shopping lists on the website show you just how you can list your ingredients according to different categories, such as meat, grocery, fridge, and so on.

Here are some other major pointers for writing your list.

* Be specific – remember if you are making two or three batches of a certain meal, you will need 2–3 times the ingredients.

* Check what you already have – this can be a money saver. Use up what you've already got, or try and pick recipes that utilise ingredients that you already have. And don't think you should have enough of an ingredient if you have half a jar/container on hand; chances are you will go to use it and find there is a lot less than you think.

* Double check your list – you'll be surprised just how much you may have missed.

* Sort your list by aisle location – chances are, you know your local supermarket pretty well, but if you don't, most have a product location guide available to customers to help you find the items you're looking for.

* Source local – you can list the items you need from specialty shops such as butchers and greengrocers if you have a local supplier that can provide you with bulk buying savings. There are great benefits to buying local and buying in bulk.

* Include packaging on your list – large ziplock bags, aluminium foil rolls and trays, and plastic wrap are key parts of your Once a Month Cooking process.

Be Budget Conscious

Sticking to a budget is important when you plan your Once a Month Cooking session and choose your recipes, as economy is one of the primary goals of freezer cooking. Scan through the catalogues of specials at your local supermarkets and keep an eye out for weekly deals at local specialty stores. Stick to your list too; regardless of whether canned tomatoes are ridiculously cheap this week, your list only says six cans so you only get six cans. Set the budget for your shopping trip and allow just a small amount over this to cover any unexpected price rises. The best way to do this is estimate what each item on your list will cost. You will probably have a rough idea of prices from previous shopping trips so go through your list and come up with a figure. Withdraw cash from the bank and only spend that amount. It's surprising how much more carefully you shop if you are only carrying cash. Don't be afraid to take a calculator with you when you shop either; you'd be surprised how easily you can go over your budget when you pop one or two 'extra' items in the trolley.

GET YOUR KITCHEN ORGANISED

Before you start to cook, you need to make sure you have everything to cook in and with. When you are looking through your recipes, keep in mind which utensils and cookware you will need. These are likely to include:

* pots
* pans
* casserole dishes
* baking trays
* strainer
* wooden spoon
* ladle
* slow cooker or two
* sharp knife
* vegetable peeler

In fact, just about everything in your kitchen will be needed on cooking day! To make things easier and to save you from buying new dishes and trays, borrow from family and friends. But remember to only borrow items that are similar in size and shape to yours, so when it comes to defrosting and cooking you don't have to re-borrow the same dish. Another great tip is to borrow a slow cooker from someone so you can have a couple of meals on the go at the same time.

The other thing to check you have enough of is the equipment you need to freeze your meals. Make sure you have on hand:

* ziplock bags
* plastic wrap
* aluminium foil
* aluminium foil containers (with cardboard lids)
* permanent markers

For the ziplock bags, make sure they are high quality and specifically state on the box that they are 'freezer quality'. You don't want to open your freezer door to find that one of the bags has split and there's a large puddle of soup rapidly solidifying on the freezer floor!

Okay. The recipes have been scrutinised, the meals have been planned, the list has been made and you've got all the gear to get started. Time to go shopping!

Shopping

Once you have planned your shopping list, you need to plan your shop. Shopping efficiently saves time, money and energy. It's beneficial to plan your shopping day when you will be able to take care of purchasing everything, a day or two in advance of your chosen cooking day (a week is too long for, say, certain meats to sit in your fridge before you cook them, especially meat on sale – you can never trust that for more than a day or two, but make sure you check the use-by date). Equally, you should never try to schedule your shopping for the same day as the cooking.

Tip from a SAHM

When I shop online I arrange the order by 'lowest price first' so it is easy to compare prices. *SARAH HINDE*

If you can, shop without the kids. As much as we love them, kids can be a huge distraction when you are shopping on a tight schedule and to a precise list. And you won't have them pestering you to buy any extras. Make sure you have plenty of bags and either some freezer bags or an esky for the cold goods. Plan to shop first thing in the morning when the shops open because they are usually fairly quiet then. Alternatively, shop late at night when meat and fresh produce are often marked down in price.

OUT IN THE FIELD (SO TO SPEAK)

Your list is your bible on shopping day. Keep it with you at all times and carry a pen to mark off the items as you get them. You've done your research so stick to your plan and try not to second-guess yourself.

Keep your eyes open for specials and discounts, but only purchase these items if you are sure they provide a significant saving compared to the original choice. Put promotional prices on your list as you see them so you can compare if you find something you think is a better deal.

Stay focused and only buy what is on your list. It's easy to waste time strolling the aisles.

The major supermarket chains offer online grocery delivery, which can be very handy. You can order what is on your list and not be tempted by extras and bargains offered in store, and the produce is delivered to your door. This can save a significant amount of time, as you will only have to visit specialty stores and suppliers for extra ingredients. You do however need to check if they deliver in your area and place your order a couple of days ahead to ensure delivery times co-ordinate with your cooking day. You may also need to pay a delivery fee, which will impact on your budget.

Markets and Wholesale Warehouses

Markets are a great way to save money on bulk vegetables and fruit (and sometimes even meat, depending on where you go). You can talk to the supplier about the quality and quantities, and you may even be able to organise a regular delivery of assorted fruit and vegetables direct to your home.

Similarly, bulk suppliers are a convenient way to pick up huge quantities of produce for a much reduced per-unit price. Familiarise yourself with the usual price per unit at supermarkets to compare.

Meat and Poultry

The meat and poultry portion of your shopping list will be the biggest expense, so try to find specials and deals on the cuts you need. Your local butcher may give a discount for bulk orders and can package in quantities that you request, but supermarkets are also able to wrap selected meats and chicken in any weight you need. It is vital to know just how much you need of each ingredient so as to avoid food wastage and over-spending, so watch your quantities and keep an eye out for cheaper alternatives. For instance, casserole beef or chuck steak is ideal for slow cooker recipes and costs a fraction of the price of prime steak, while chicken thigh fillets tend to be cheaper and more versatile than breasts, and are more tender upon defrosting.

Frozen Vegetables

If you're buying frozen vegetables, check to make sure that the contents haven't been defrosted and re-frozen. Gently squeeze the bag. If the contents move freely and easily then they have not been defrosted. If the contents are in one big lump it suggests they've been re-frozen.

Tips

In true frugal style, keep an eye on the register as your shopping is being checked out to make sure the correct prices are being charged, and check your receipt before leaving the store. Keep your receipts in a file at home. If you find an item is out of date, spoilt or rancid, don't just throw it away; take the item (and receipt) back to the store for a replacement, refund or credit. Keeping the receipt also provides you with a record of the cost of items for your next Once a Month Cooking shopping list.

BRINGING HOME THE BACON

When you get back home with your shopping, get all the cold foods (meats especially) straight into the fridge. Put all the remaining foods together in a single place, be it in a corner of the kitchen counter or a cupboard designated specifically for that purpose. That way you won't need to search multiple places to find everything you need on cooking day, and you reduce the risk of family members using anything before you cook it.

As you unpack, check that nothing has been left out. It is easy, when you find that one shop is out of stock of a product, to make a mental note to pick it up elsewhere, but then simply forget. It's a good idea to print out two lists, one to take and one to check off when you get home. If anything has been forgotten, head back out and get it as soon as possible.

Finally, before you start cooking, empty out the freezer. This is, after all, where all the fruits of your labour will end up so you need to make sure it has enough room available for storage.

Cooking

The big day is here at last! Just think, after today no more cooking for the rest of the month! If that's not worth the time, I don't know what is. I'm going to give you all the tips I have to make this day as efficient as possible.

Have all your recipes printed out or marked ready to go. Familiarise yourself with your recipes and make sure you fully understand the processes involved in each one. There is nothing worse than leaving a recipe you thought was simple and quick to the very last only to read that it actually needs to refrigerate for an extended period or involves a process that takes a lot of time and effort (not a great idea at the end of a big day of cooking!). Make sure you have a clean kitchen and enough utensils to work with. Any mess or clutter will hinder your progress. It's also a good idea to clean periodically throughout the day. It's probably necessary, in fact – I don't know about you but I don't own seven casserole dishes, so I need to wash mine between recipes. If you own a dishwasher you can place the dirty dishes in as you go and then turn it on once it gets full.

Before you get stuck in, it's also important to get comfy! You're going to be on your feet and in the same room of the house all day so it's best you are dressed for the occasion and prepare your environment accordingly. Make sure you are wearing comfortable shoes and clothes, ensure you have an easy lunch and snacks on hand and crank up some tunes!

DO YOUR PREPARATION IN BULK

Begin by taking care of all of the prep. If you have multiple recipes that call for diced onions, dice them all at once and then divide into portions for each recipe. I leave a section in my fridge where I can put the prepared ingredients I don't need immediately. As I prepare ingredients, I group everything together by recipe, not by food type. Label each bowl with the recipe name and the amount of the ingredient in the bowl. This is also a good time to cook any meat that has to be pre-cooked or browned for a recipe. Again, use the same labelling system in the refrigerator to keep your bowl of 450 grams of beef separate from the bowl of 550 grams of beef that is for a different recipe.

MAKE YOUR STEWS AND CASSEROLES FIRST

After the ingredient preparation is complete I work on all of my 'long cookers' – soups, stews, casseroles and anything that requires several hours of cooking time and minimal maintenance. Put the stews on a back burner on the stovetop (or in the slow cooker) and get into your other recipes while they cook away.

If you are using a slow cooker, to save space it is often a good idea to prepare and combine the ingredients in your kitchen, put them in the cooker, then put it in another room of the house. Just be sure to keep it up off the floor, away from bench edges and check on it regularly. I like to put mine in the laundry so I can check on it on the way to the loo during the day.

Now, some people find it challenging to work on multiple recipes simultaneously. It's true; it can be very difficult to do, especially since cooking can be a delicate process. If this is the way you are then go ahead and use your own method for cooking. It's better to cook for a few extra hours than to burn every other dish you try to prepare. Another tip is to leave post-it notes near the food that is cooking so you know the next step. If your memory is really bad, grab a cheap kitchen timer to help you.

Do not add uncooked, un-defrosted meat to a slow cooker or crockpot; the risk of the meat not cooking properly during the slow cooking process is too high. Cook the meat, make up the casserole and freeze as a whole to save time and minimise the chance of food poisoning.

SANDWICHES

Alongside your cooking, you might also choose to make two week's worth of sandwiches. Then you can just pop them in the kids' lunch boxes every day.

To make sure your sandwiches freeze well:

* Make sure the bread is extremely fresh. Most bread actually freezes very well, although steer clear of wraps or tortillas if you can – these tend to get very brittle in the freezer and you're more likely to end up with a broken mess. I think seeded bread and wholemeal or multigrain bread tend to fare better in the freezer as they are more 'dense' – and they're a lot better for you.

* Ensure the sandwich is well wrapped. The best wrapping is plastic wrap, as it doesn't allow air to circulate around the bread, which would make it stale. Sandwiches also thaw better when in plastic wrap. I do not recommend ziplock bags for freezing sandwiches or even airtight containers.

* Place the sandwich on a flat surface in the freezer and avoid the white plastic racks if you can. Sometimes the sandwiches can 'fall through the gaps' and become a funny shape – then they won't fit in the lunch box!

* Make sure you note on the wrapping the type of sandwich and the date it was made. I would not recommend freezing sandwiches more than 2 weeks in advance.

Fillings that work well

* meats such as cooked chicken (chopped), ham, roast beef, roast pork, turkey, salami, meatballs
* canned salmon and tuna
* peanut butter, Nutella and most nut butters
* butter (firm, not melted, or it will make the bread soggy)
* cream cheese
* grated cheese (cheese slices don't work well, so if you want to freeze it, grate it first)
* mayonnaise
* pickles, chutneys and relishes
* sundried tomatoes (finely chopped)
* Vegemite
* jam

(Condiments such as mayonnaise can make the bread soggy before freezing, so create your sandwich with the wettest ingredients in the centre.)

Fillings that should be avoided

* fresh tomato
* lettuce
* egg (especially egg white – it gets very rubbery on defrosting)
* fresh vegetables
* anything that has a high water content, such as cucumbers and fresh onion (in fact, most salad ingredients don't freeze well)

BLANCHING VEGETABLES

Another extra thing you can do on your cooking day is blanch and freeze vegetables. It's quick and easy, and means you can have vegies on hand all the time to add to dishes or as a side. The basic idea with blanching vegetables is that you boil them briefly and drop them in ice water to stop them overcooking. This preserves their bright colours and crispy-yet-tender texture.

Place ice and water (enough to cover all your vegetables) into a bowl. Fill a large saucepan with water and bring to the boil. Meanwhile, chop the vegetables into evenly sized pieces. How big is up to you. Just before you put the vegetables in, put a few pinches of salt into the boiling water. You don't have to do this, but it helps the vegetables keep their flavour.

Put the vegetables in the boiling water in batches so the water never gets below a boil. If you're blanching more than one type of vegetable, keep each one separate so the flavours don't mix. You might want to go from lightest to darkest, because darker vegetables can tint the water and stain the other vegies. After 30 seconds, remove one piece, dunk it in a bowl of ice water, and give it a taste. If it's cooked enough, take out all of the vegies. If not, give it another 30 seconds. When they're ready, use a slotted spoon to transfer to the bowl of ice water. After the vegies cool down, scoop them out of the bowl and drain on a plate lined with paper towel. Cool to room temperature, seal in a ziplock bag and freeze for up to 3 months. You don't need to thaw them, just add to a pan of boiling water to reheat.

Freezing

Many of us already practise freezer cooking in a smaller way. Have you ever cooked up a double batch of chicken to have some for dinner and some for lunch the next day? Or made more than your family's share of spaghetti sauce or lasagne and put it in the freezer for another day? It's not much harder to cook double or triple amounts of your recipes, but what exactly is suitable to freeze and what isn't? Fortunately, most foods are freezable. There are a few, however, that shouldn't be frozen. These include:

* food in cans
* raw food with a high water content (such a salad ingredients)
* foods that have been frozen and defrosted (but it's okay if you cook them before refreezing, e.g. frozen pastry and frozen mince)
* dishes that have been cooked, frozen and reheated
* most raw fruit and vegetables
* fresh 'soft' herbs such as parsley, basil and chives (unless processed)

Almost every other foodstuff can be frozen. See page 216 for a table that outlines the freezing times and methods for many common foods.

FREEZER STORAGE BASICS

When freezing, the biggest thing to remember is to properly and accurately label everything in the freezer. When possible, use a permanent marker to note:

* the name of the recipe
* the date it was frozen
* the use-by date
* the size of the dish it was cooked in (if you know the pan size, you can easily pop it back in for reheating)

By putting the name of the recipe on the label you can quickly check back on the cooking instructions to see how to reheat it. It is also a great idea to write down the meals that you have in the freezer, and the quantity. This is so you know what is on hand, and you can have your family choose what to eat the next day. Plus, then you know when meals are getting low, and you need to plan your next Once a Month cook-up.

If you remember your basic physics, you'll know that cold air moves downward. Because of this, food on the bottom of the freezer will freeze fastest, so what I do is let the food freeze on the bottom first and then move it to a higher shelf. Soups, stews, and sauces I place into ziplock bags and lay flat on the bottom shelf. They freeze into conveniently stackable layers that can be piled up like bricks, saving space. Try to group items that are similarly shaped so that you don't leave large air pockets between them.

FREEZER STORAGE TIMES

Because freezing keeps most foods safe for consumption for an indefinite amount of time (providing the freezer functions adequately, they are stored correctly, the right types of foods are frozen and correct temperatures are adhered to), recommended freezer storage times are a guide only. Quality and edibility of defrosted foods should be determined upon thawing by checking smell and appearance. Some foods develop a rancid odour when frozen too long, and some may separate as they freeze; these foods should be discarded. The appearance of some foods can change as they freeze, but they can be perfectly fine to eat. Be sure to check if these changes are normal before you throw out a perfectly good product. Those that no longer look appetising may not be suitable to serve as a main dish, but can be incorporated as a side or have other ingredients added to them.

Refer to the freezer storage chart on page 216 to find the recommended freezing times for best quality.

THAWING

The main factor in making sure your frozen food is safe and at its best is the thawing method. When food is not defrosted correctly – at the wrong temperature or left for too long – bacteria can breed and food poisoning can occur. The best method for thawing is in the fridge overnight and the larger the frozen food package, the longer the defrosting time. The food needs to be stored on the bottom shelf of the fridge as this is not only the coldest part but the lowest, which means any liquid coming from the defrosting food cannot drip onto other foods and contaminate them.

It can be tempting to leave frozen meat on the draining board or in the sink to defrost throughout the day. However, this can be dangerous as the temperature level in your home can fluctuate and cause bacterial growth if the defrosting food gets too warm.

For faster thawing (for those of us who frequently forget to take something out of the freezer for dinner), place the food in a large, leak-proof plastic bag and immerse it in cold water. Do not use hot water as this promotes bacteria growth. Do not place the food directly into your kitchen sink without a bag to protect it, as it can be contaminated by bacteria in the sink, or vice versa. Check the water frequently to be sure it stays cold, and change it every 30 minutes. Cook the food immediately after it has thawed.

When using the microwave to defrost food, cook it immediately after thawing. Microwaves are notorious for not heating food evenly and some parts of the food may have already started to cook during microwaving.

FREEZER BURN

Freezer burn does not make food unsafe, just dry in spots. Freezer burn occurs when food is dehydrated by coming into contact with the air in your freezer. It appears as a grey-brown, leathery area and can look very unappetising. Freezer-burned areas of food are more likely to have an 'off' flavour and a tougher texture. The main cause of freezer burn is a lack of airtight packaging but there are other contributing factors, including:

* freezer temperature set too high
* fluctuating freezer temperature caused by opening and shutting the door and placing hot food into the freezer
* wrong sized food packaging – containers should leave a little room for expansion but that's it; too much space around the food in the container increases the risk of freezer burn
* not pushing enough air out of the packaging before freezing
* not accurately labelling and dating food – the longer a food is frozen, the more susceptible it is to freezer burn

To minimise the likelihood of freezer burn, wrap your food tightly in plastic wrap or place in a ziplock bag, ensuring as much excess air is pushed out as possible. Allow a small amount of room for expansion and seal tightly. The same goes for plastic containers – make sure all lids have seals intact and the container is at least three-quarters full in its liquid state (it will expand on freezing).

Freezer-burned areas may rehydrate somewhat on thawing and cooking, but it is best to cut them away either before or after cooking as they can be more susceptible to contamination and spoiling. Heavily freezer-burned foods should be discarded, as their quality is usually quite poor.

Quick Tips

✳ **COOL FOOD:** Freezing food when hot will only increase the temperature of the freezer and could cause other food to start defrosting. Leave your dishes to cool to room temperature before placing them into the freezer.

✳ **FILL THE FREEZER:** A full freezer is more efficient and economical to run, as the cold air does not have as much room to circulate. If you have lots of free space even after doing your freezer cooking, or as you use your meals, half fill plastic bottles with water and pack them around the items in the freezer.

✳ **PORTION CONTROL:** Freeze food in portions. Aim for both family sized and single serve portions; some nights you may only have one or two family members home for dinner and some nights you will have the whole family plus extras. Freezing different sized portions eliminates wastage and also provides backups for lunches when there are no leftovers. Smaller servings also thaw faster.

✳ **GET OUT WHAT YOU PUT IN:** Don't freeze old food just to save on food waste; freezing does not improve the quality of produce. The point of freezing is to keep food at its prime, so try to cook and freeze it as soon as possible after you purchase it.

It's all in the planning! Plan the monthly menu, set a budget and make a list. You'll have three main groups: fresh fruit and veg, packaged food and staples from your pantry.

Cooking

You don't need fancy equipment to cook in bulk. My favourite things are my slow cooker (an engagement present from years ago!) and my stick blender.

Share your cooking day with a friend – it doesn't have to be a chore. This is Lydia, Stay at Home Mum's food editor.

Be organised with the chopping. For example, chop all the onion needed for the recipes you're cooking and divide it into the portions required.

Get the slow-cooker dishes on first so that you don't have to think about them till the end of the day. This chook was slow-cooked then browned in the oven. Yum!

Packaging and Labelling

Lasagne is a family favourite and it freezes beautifully. Cook, assemble, label, freeze and there's dinner ready to go. Cook double the quantity of meat in a slow cooker and you'll have plenty for bolognaise as well.

One of the biggest things to remember is to accurately label everything that goes in the freezer.

Freezing

Start off just cooking a week's worth of dinners if you have a small freezer. That's how I started, then when I could afford it I bought a big upright freezer. It's been the best investment ever.

Make sure you have a good variety of containers on hand. You'll soon work out what works best for your family.

Date: March 2014
Contents: Mini Potato Bake

Having lots of things packaged in single serves makes dinner and school lunches so much easier.

BANANA BREAD

Dinner's Ready!

Within minutes
I can feed my boys
something healthy,
quick and filling for
dinner. Everyone
is happy!

Quick Tips (continued)

✶ **IF IN DOUBT, THROW IT OUT:** If you find something lurking at the bottom of your freezer and there are no identifiable signs as to what it is, throw it out. The same applies if you defrost something and the smell or appearance seems odd.

✶ **LABELS ARE YOUR FRIENDS:** Labelling your freezer cooking may seem time-consuming after you have spent so much time cooking everything, but it will save you the guesswork when it comes to identifying what is in every package. You can include cooking instructions and ingredients if you are cooking for guests (to avoid any allergic reactions) or family while you are away.

✶ **FREEZER MAINTENANCE:** Too much ice in any freezer makes it inefficient and can lead to motor damage, so make sure you defrost your freezer if ice builds up. Invest in a freezer thermometer to ensure the freezer temperature does not fluctuate too much (or drop below −17°C) and attend to 'funny' noises and smells immediately.

✶ **IN AN EMERGENCY:** If you experience a power cut or you think the freezer has been shorted out, don't open the lid. The freezer will act like an esky and food should remain frozen for up to 24 hours.

✶ **REUSING DISHES:** For large casseroles, line the casserole dish you intend to cook it in with heavy aluminium foil. Cook the casserole, cool and freeze. Once frozen, remove the foil-wrapped food and seal in a ziplock bag. To reheat, simply take out of the bag and place back in the original casserole dish.

✶ **STORE THE COMPONENTS:** Some dishes incorporate ingredients that freeze really well on their own but not so much when combined. Freezing the different ingredients prepared for a specific recipe separately will still save you time; just combine when it comes to the final stages of cooking. For example, freeze a container of chicken stock and a ziplock bag of just-cooked chicken for chicken soup and add the vegetables once everything is on the stove.

✶ **STORE NOW, THICKEN LATER:** Thickened stews and gravies can separate after freezing, especially those using cornflour or plain flour to thicken. Freeze the meal first and add thickening agents while reheating.

Recipes

My Top 20 Recipes

This is a selection of dishes that I know work well for any family. They make a great starting point for Once a Month Cooking.

* Eligh's Caramelised Banana Bread – page 32

* Chicken and Cheese Soup – page 50

* Sausage Casserole – page 62

* Curried Sausages – page 64

* Bulk Bolognaise Sauce – page 68

* Savoury Mince – page 69

* Gassy Lasagne – page 70

* Chicken Pot Pie – page 88

* Chicken and Vegetable Sausages Rolls – page 97

* Beef Stroganoff – page 101

* I Can't Believe It's Not Mince Lasagne – page 115

* Sour Cream Quiche – page 121

* Bulk Savoury Muffins – page 126

* Pizza Scrolls – page 131

* Apple Turnovers – page 153

* 120 Biscuits for $7 – page 158

* Frugal Chocolate Slice – page 169

* Tim Tam Balls – page 181

* Fruit Salad Cake – page 188

* Dairy- and Egg-free Cake – page 199

Notes on Recipes

These recipes are not from a chef. They're tested and tasted at the family dinner table where the feedback is brutally honest.

Serves: unless otherwise stated, all the recipes are designed to feed a family of four. If you have a smaller family, you'll have extra portions for the fridge and, of course, you can scale up the recipes if you want to freeze more.

Brands: these recipes will work with home brand (no-name) ingredients or the best you can afford.

Garlic: some people prefer it fresh, some prefer it minced in a jar. Use either in these recipes. 1 clove of garlic = 1 teaspoon of minced garlic.

Tin sizes: the loaf tin we use is a standard 26 by 11 centimetres (2.5-litre capacity). All other cakes are made in a 22-centimetre round or square tin.

Buttermilk: wherever buttermilk is used, you can substitute the same amount of milk with white vinegar. Add 1 tablespoon of white vinegar to 1 cup of milk. Leave for a minimum of 10 minutes before use.

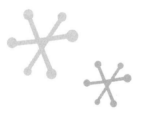

Breakfasts

My house is always mad
in the mornings. Getting the
kids up and washed and dressed,
making lunches, getting hubby out the
door, getting me out the door without
having a rat's nest for hair and this
morning's Vegemite on my face. Having
pre-prepared breakfasts on the really
mad days is great for the busy
and/or forgetful mum.

Eligh's Caramelised Banana Bread

This is Lydia's (our Stay at Home Mum food editor) son's favourite banana bread because it's dark and moist. He tells me it looks like the ones at a café, only it tastes better! Yes, you will cook it for 2 hours. Yes, you will need to line the tin with foil. No, it won't stick. Yes, your tastebuds will thank you for the wait.

3 overripe bananas

1 cup raw sugar

3 teaspoons bicarbonate of soda

pinch of salt

2 eggs, beaten

¼ cup oil

1½ cups plain flour

½ cup buttermilk

Preheat the oven to 130°C. Line a loaf tin with foil. Mash the bananas in a mixing bowl, add the sugar, bicarbonate of soda and salt. Mix well. Add the eggs and combine, then mix in the oil, then the flour, then the buttermilk. Pour into the loaf tin and bake for 2 hours, or until a skewer inserted into the centre comes out clean.

Freezing: Allow to cool to room temperature then wrap slices in plastic wrap. Freeze for up to 4 months.

Thawing: Allow to sit on the kitchen counter for 10–15 minutes.

Hints & Tips

* Store in an airtight container in the refrigerator for up to 4 days.
* I like to serve this bread with cinnamon and honey butter. Combine 100 grams of softened butter with 1 teaspoon of ground cinnamon and 2 teaspoons of honey. Mix until smooth.

Milo Banana Bread

My kids' two favourite things are bananas and Milo – put them together and you get this fantastic Milo Banana Bread that is full of energy and goodness.

4 ripe bananas

¼ cup oil

1 teaspoon vanilla
essence

1 teaspoon bicarbonate
of soda

¾ cup almond meal

¾ cup plain flour

1 cup Milo

3 eggs

⅓ cup milk

Preheat the oven to 180°C. Line a loaf tin with baking paper. In a large bowl, mash the bananas then add the oil, vanilla essence and bicarbonate of soda. Mix well using a wooden spoon. Add the almond meal, flour and Milo, mix well with wooden spoon. Place the eggs and milk into a separate bowl and whisk with a fork until lightly beaten. Pour into the banana mixture and stir to combine. Pour into the loaf tin and bake for 50–60 minutes, or until golden brown and a skewer inserted into the centre comes out clean. Cool in the tin for 10 minutes before turning onto a wire rack to cool completely.

Freezing: Allow to cool to room temperature, cut into slices and double wrap in plastic wrap. Freeze for up to 4 months.

Thawing: Allow to sit on the kitchen counter for 10–15 minutes.

Hints & Tips

* Keep in an airtight container in the refrigerator for up to 4 days.
* Can also be made into cupcakes. Divide between the holes of a 12-hole muffin tin lined with paper cases, and bake for 30 minutes.

Fig, Apricot and Walnut Bread

Fig, Apricot and Walnut Bread is a moist and heavy loaf that is great toasted for breakfast or wrapped, still warm, in a tea towel as a gift for someone who has everything!

1 × 7 g sachet dried yeast

2 tablespoons honey or molasses

1 cup warm water

200 g dried figs, roughly chopped

100 g dried apricots, roughly chopped

1 cup walnuts, roughly chopped

1¼ cups plain flour

1¼ cups wholemeal flour

2 teaspoons mixed spice

pinch of salt

Preheat the oven to 180°C. Grease a loaf tin well with butter. Place the yeast, honey or molasses and warm water in a bowl and mix to combine. Leave in a warm place for 10 minutes or until foamy. Add the figs, apricots and walnuts. Sift the flours, mixed spice and salt together and fold into the yeast mixture. Turn out onto a floured surface and knead until smooth (about 10 minutes). Place the dough into an oiled bowl, cover with plastic wrap and leave in a warm place for 2 hours, or until the dough has doubled in size. Punch down the dough and knead for a further 5 minutes. Press the dough into the tin and let it rise again for 30 minutes. Bake for 45 minutes, or until the loaf sounds hollow when tapped. Leave in the tin for 10 minutes before eating warm with slabs of butter.

Freezing: Cut the cooled bread into serving slices then wrap in plastic wrap. Freeze for up to 2 months.

Thawing: Can be popped frozen straight into the toaster or a lunch box. Alternatively, allow to sit on the kitchen counter for 10 minutes.

Reheating: If you want to warm the bread, toast until a nice crust forms.

Strawberry Bread

Strawberry Bread is a great breakfast, but also works as an afternoon snack. It's best served warm, with lashings of butter or maybe some golden syrup, if you're feeling particularly naughty.

250 g strawberries

½ cup brown sugar

½ cup light olive oil

1 egg

1½ cups self-raising flour, sifted

½ cup milk

Preheat the oven to 170°C. Lightly grease a loaf tin and line with baking paper. Thinly slice half the strawberries and cut the remainder into halves. Place the sugar, oil and egg into a medium bowl. Beat with an electric mixer on high for 5–8 minutes, or until thick and creamy. Fold in the flour alternately with the milk, then fold in the sliced berries. Spread the mixture into the loaf tin and top with the halved strawberries. Bake for 55 minutes, or until a skewer inserted into the centre comes out clean. Allow to stand in the tin for 10 minutes then turn onto a wire rack to cool.

Freezing: Cut the cooled bread into serving slices and wrap in plastic wrap. Freeze for up to 2 months.

Thawing: Can be popped frozen straight into the toaster or a lunch box. Alternatively, allow to sit on the kitchen counter for 5 minutes.

Reheating: If you want to warm the bread, toast until a nice crust forms.

Hints & Tips

* Store in an airtight container in the fridge for up to 3 days.

Breakfast Muffins

Need a fast breakfast on the go? Then make a batch of these Breakfast Muffins; they freeze beautifully so you will always have a decent start to the day at hand.

canola oil spray

1¾ cups wholemeal self-raising flour

1 teaspoon cinnamon

½ cup caster sugar

1½ cups low-fat muesli

80 g low-fat olive oil spread

1 cup reduced-fat Greek yoghurt

2 eggs

2 red apples, peeled and grated

1 tablespoon honey

Preheat the oven to 180°C. Grease a 12-hole muffin tin well with canola oil spray. Sift the flour and cinnamon together in a bowl and then add the caster sugar and muesli and mix well. In a separate bowl, mix together the olive oil spread, yoghurt and eggs until well combined. Pour slowly into the dry ingredients and stir with a wooden spoon until just combined. Add the grated apple and stir to combine. Pour into the muffin tin and drizzle the honey over the top. Bake for 20 minutes. Allow to cool in the tin for 10 minutes, then turn onto a wire rack.

* *

Freezing: Allow to cool then place in a ziplock bag. Freeze for up to 2 months.

Thawing: Pop into lunch boxes frozen. Alternatively, allow to sit on the kitchen counter for 5 minutes.

Reheating: If you want your muffins to be hot, heat in the microwave for 8 seconds each.

Bran Muffins

Want a healthy muffin recipe? Bran Muffins are both filling and good for you. They also keep you regular!

1 cup bran

½ cup olive oil

1 cup white sugar

½ cup brown sugar

3¾ cups plain flour

2½ teaspoons bicarbonate of soda

pinch of salt

2 cups milk

2 eggs, beaten

1 cup sultanas

Preheat the oven to 200°C. Line a 12-hole muffin tin with paper cases. Soak the bran in 1 cup of boiling water for 5 minutes. Beat the oil and sugars together until well combined. Add the bran and water. Sift the flour, bicarbonate of soda and salt together in a separate bowl. In another bowl, combine the milk and eggs. Add to the bran, alternating with the flour mixture. Stir in the sultanas then divide between the holes in the muffin tin. Bake for 20–25 minutes, until golden. Allow to cool in the tin for 10 minutes, then turn onto a wire rack.

* *

Freezing: Allow the muffins to cool. Place in a ziplock bag and freeze for up to 2 months. Take out individual muffins as required.

Thawing: Pop into lunch boxes frozen. Alternatively, allow to sit on the kitchen counter for 5 minutes.

Reheating: If you want your muffins to be hot, heat in the microwave for 8 seconds each.

Bacon and Egg Toasted Muffins

Bacon and Egg Toasted Muffins are super delicious and so much fun to make.

canola oil spray

6 rashers bacon

6 slices bread

2 teaspoons butter

200 g cheddar cheese, grated

6 eggs

Preheat the oven to 180°C. Grease a 6-hole muffin tin with canola oil spray. Quickly fry the bacon until just cooked. Using a cookie cutter, cut rounds from the bread and spread with butter. Press into the greased muffin tin and divide the cheese evenly over the six muffins. Make the bacon into a 'ring' and place upright on top of the bread. Pop into the oven for approximately 4 minutes, or until the cheese has melted and the bacon is crisp. Carefully break an egg into the centre of each muffin (pour off some egg white if there is too much) and bake in the oven for approximately 10 minutes, or until the egg yolk is set. Serve hot fresh from the oven.

Freezing: Wrap each muffin in a paper towel, then plastic wrap. Freeze for up to 2 weeks.

Thawing: Allow to sit on the kitchen counter for 10 minutes.

Reheating: Pop into a toaster oven or microwave and cook until heated through.

Traditional Pancakes

Whip up these pancakes for the perfect start to the weekend. Serve with honey, yoghurt, berries, figs or chocolate syrup – or a combination. But be warned, these pancakes are seriously addictive!

75 g butter, plus extra to cook

1¼ cups milk

1 cup buttermilk

1 egg

1 teaspoon vanilla essence

2 cups plain flour

3 teaspoons baking powder

½ cup caster sugar

Melt the butter in a bowl in the microwave then add the milk, buttermilk, egg and vanilla and whisk together until well combined. Sift all dry ingredients into a mixing bowl. Pour in the wet mixture gradually, whisking continuously. Cook in batches in a frying pan over medium heat, adding a small slice of butter to each batch.

* *

Freezing: Allow to cool then stack between sheets of baking paper and place in an airtight container. Freeze for up to 2 weeks.

Thawing: Allow to sit on the kitchen counter for 5 minutes.

Reheating: Either microwave the pancakes until warm, or pop them in the toaster.

Hints & Tips

* If you don't have buttermilk to hand, use an extra ¾ cup of milk.
* Use cookie cutters to create a theme for your breakfast, by cutting out shapes from the cooked pancakes.

Soups

Soup is a quick, easy, healthy and filling dinner or lunch in the winter months. Served with some hot cheesy toast, it's a meal you can have on the table in 10 minutes flat.

Pea and Ham Soup

Pea and Ham Soup is a winter staple in my house. I make a huge batch at the beginning of winter and freeze in single servings. Sometimes hubby takes a serve for lunch with a crusty bread roll.

1 × 500 g packet green or yellow split peas

1 ham hock

2 brown onions, chopped

2 carrots, chopped

2 potatoes or sweet potatoes, chopped

2 sticks celery, chopped

salt and pepper

Rinse the split peas and soak them in water in the fridge overnight. Discard the water and place in a deep pot or slow cooker. Add the ham hock and cover with fresh water. Cook on high for 4 hours. Add the vegetables to the slow cooker, turn it onto low, and cook for another 4 hours, or until the peas have melted and the hock is starting to fall apart. Using tongs, remove the ham hock from the soup and remove and discard the skin. Chop the ham into chunky pieces and add back to the slow cooker. Season with salt and pepper to taste.

Freezing: Allow to cool to room temperature then three-quarters fill a ziplock bag and store on a flat surface. Freeze for up to 6 months.

Thawing: Allow to sit in the fridge overnight.

Reheating: Place in a saucepan to heat through or reheat in the microwave, stirring every minute, until hot.

Cauliflower Cheese Soup

Everyone loves cauliflower cheese – and now you can have it as a soup!

3 cups vegetable stock

1 large cauliflower, diced

1 × 425 g can cream of chicken soup

1 cup grated tasty cheese

1 teaspoon garlic salt

fresh parsley, to serve

Place the stock in a large pot over medium–high heat and bring to the boil. Add the cauliflower and boil for a further 5 minutes. Add the remaining ingredients and reduce the heat to low. Simmer for 40 minutes. Serve with a sprig of parsley in each bowl.

Freezing: Allow to cool to room temperature then three-quarters fill a ziplock bag and store on a flat surface. Freeze for up to 6 months.

Thawing: Allow to sit in the fridge overnight.

Reheating: Place in a saucepan to heat through or reheat in the microwave, stirring every minute, until hot.

Hints & Tips

* Keep refrigerated for up to 3 days in an airtight container.

Creamy Vegetable Soup

A delicious vegetarian soup for the colder winter months.

45 g butter

1 leek, chopped

¼ cup plain flour

5 cups water

2 vegetable stock cubes

1 potato, peeled and chopped into chunks

2 carrots, peeled and chopped

1 head broccoli, cut into small florets

2 zucchini, sliced

½ cup cream

salt and pepper

In a large saucepan, melt the butter until bubbling. Add the leek and cook until soft. Stir in the flour and cook the mixture, stirring with a wooden spoon, until thick. Add the water, stock cubes and potato. Cook for about 5 minutes before adding the remaining vegetables. Simmer for 10 minutes, or until the vegetables are cooked through. Stir in the cream, season with salt and pepper to taste, and serve immediately.

Freezing: Allow to cool to room temperature then three-quarters fill a ziplock bag and store on a flat surface. Freeze for up to 6 months.

Thawing: Allow to sit in the fridge overnight.

Reheating: Place in a saucepan to heat through or reheat in the microwave, stirring every minute, until hot.

Hints & Tips

* You can substitute a brown onion for the leek, if you prefer.

Roast Chicken and Garlic Soup

Forget chicken noodle soup – if you're sick or under the weather, this hearty and healthy Roast Chicken and Garlic Soup is for you! Don't be alarmed at the amount of garlic; when baked it caramelises and mellows. The end result is a taste sensation.

1 kg chicken breast

2 tablespoons olive oil

salt and pepper

20 cloves garlic

1 brown onion, finely diced

½ bunch celery, finely diced

2 carrots, finely diced

2 teaspoons freshly grated ginger

3 cups chicken stock

Preheat the oven to 180°C. Line a baking tray with baking paper. Spread the chicken breasts evenly over the tray, drizzle with 1 tablespoon of the olive oil and season with salt and pepper to taste. Separate the garlic cloves but leave their skin on. Scatter on the baking tray with the chicken breasts. Bake for 20 minutes, or until the chicken is just cooked through and the garlic is baked and caramelised. Allow to cool slightly then slice the chicken into bite-sized pieces. Gently squeeze the garlic cloves – the cooked centres will 'pop' out of their jackets. Set aside. In a large saucepan, heat the remaining olive oil gently. Fry the onion, celery, carrot and ginger until they start to colour. Add the chicken stock and simmer on a very low heat for 10 minutes. Add the chicken pieces and garlic and heat for another few minutes.

Freezing: Allow to cool to room temperature then three-quarters fill a ziplock bag and store on a flat surface. Freeze for up to 6 months.

Thawing: Allow to sit in the fridge overnight.

Reheating: Place in a saucepan to heat through or reheat in the microwave, stirring every minute, until hot.

Gluten-free French Onion Soup

*We love our slow cooker recipes at SAHM and here's one that is also gluten-
and egg-free! Perfect for those cold nights in, or even as a take-to-work lunch.*

2 large brown onions

2 large white onions

2 large red onions

4 cloves garlic, crushed

2 tablespoons extra
virgin olive oil

4 cups chicken stock

4 cups beef stock

2 teaspoons chopped
fresh parsley

2 teaspoons fresh
thyme leaves

1 bay leaf

1 teaspoon salt

½ teaspoon balsamic
vinegar

6–8 slices gluten-free
bread

2 cups grated tasty
cheese

Peel and cut the onions into half moons (cut in
half then sliced) and place in the slow cooker.
Add the garlic and drizzle with the oil. Cover and
cook on high for 8 hours. Place the chicken and
beef stocks in the microwave or on the stovetop
and heat through. Add to the onions in the slow
cooker. Sprinkle the parsley and thyme in and
add the bay leaf. Cover and cook for a further
20 minutes. Remove the bay leaf, then add the
salt and balsamic vinegar. Just before serving the
soup, preheat your grill and toast the slices of
bread. Sprinkle with cheese and toast again until
the cheese has melted. Ladle the soup into bowls
and top with the cheese toasts. Serve immediately.

Freezing: Allow to cool to room temperature then
three-quarters fill a ziplock bag and store on a flat
surface. Freeze for up to 6 months.

Thawing: Allow to sit in the fridge overnight.

Reheating: Place in a saucepan to heat through
or reheat in the microwave, stirring every minute,
until hot.

Thai Pumpkin Soup

This Thai Pumpkin Soup is much better than the takeaway version, and very easy to make.

1 teaspoon sesame oil

1 tablespoon olive oil

2 onions, diced

2 teaspoons garlic salt

1 kg pumpkin, diced

2 cups chicken stock

1 × 400 ml can coconut cream

1 lime, juice and zest

2 tablespoons fish sauce

1 tablespoon brown sugar

⅓ cup chopped lemongrass

2 small red chillies, chopped

⅓ cup coriander leaves

Heat the oils in a large saucepan and lightly fry the onion and garlic salt. Add the pumpkin, stock and 2 cups water. Bring to the boil then reduce the heat and simmer for 30 minutes. Add the coconut cream, lime juice and zest, fish sauce, sugar, lemongrass and chilli. Blend with a stick mixer then simmer for 10 minutes. Serve sprinkled with coriander.

Freezing: Allow to cool to room temperature then three-quarters fill a ziplock bag and store on a flat surface. Freeze for up to 6 months.

Thawing: Allow to sit in the fridge overnight.

Reheating: Place in a saucepan to heat through or reheat in the microwave, stirring every minute, until hot.

Hints & Tips

∗ Keep refrigerated for up to 4 days in an airtight container.

Bacon and Potato Soup

Bacon and Potato Soup is another great winter dish – perfect for warming your belly on a cold night. It freezes really well so make a huge batch and you'll always have some on hand!

4 rashers rindless bacon, diced

2 tablespoons olive oil

1 leek, trimmed, halved and thinly sliced

2 cloves garlic, crushed (optional)

750 g potatoes, peeled and chopped

1 litre chicken stock

¼ cup cream

salt and pepper

¼ cup chopped chives

Cook the bacon in a large saucepan over medium–high heat for 5 minutes, or until crispy. Remove to a plate lined with paper towel. Add the oil, leek and garlic, if using, to the saucepan. Cook, stirring, for 3 minutes or until the leek is soft. Add the potatoes and stir to coat. Add the chicken stock, cover, and bring to the boil. Reduce the heat to low and simmer, partially covered, for 20 minutes, or until the potatoes are tender. Blend with a stick mixer then return to the saucepan. Add the cream and three-quarters of the cooked bacon. Stir over low heat until the soup is heated through. Season with salt and pepper to taste. Sprinkle with the remaining bacon and chopped chives.

Freezing: Allow to cool to room temperature then three-quarters fill a ziplock bag and store on a flat surface. Freeze for up to 6 months.

Thawing: Allow to sit in the fridge overnight.

Reheating: Place in a saucepan to heat through or reheat in the microwave, stirring every minute, until hot.

Rustic Tomato Soup

Rustic Tomato Soup tastes nothing like nails! It's a brilliant soup recipe that I really love. It's a great way to use up any excess tomatoes when they are in season – and it freezes beautifully.

2 kg ripe tomatoes, chopped

1 large onion, chopped

2 tablespoons sugar

½ cup water

pinch of baking soda

salt

2 tablespoons cornflour

½ cup milk

Place the tomatoes, onion, sugar and water into a large saucepan. Bring to the boil and simmer for approximately 1 hour. Strain through a sieve or sauce strainer to remove the tomato skins and seeds, then return the liquid to the saucepan and reheat. Add the baking soda and mix well. Season with salt to taste. In a small bowl, mix together the cornflour and milk to make a smooth paste. Stir into the soup before it comes to the boil and then remove from the heat.

Freezing: Allow to cool to room temperature then three-quarters fill a ziplock bag and store on a flat surface. Freeze for up to 6 months.

Thawing: Allow to sit in the fridge overnight.

Reheating: Place in a saucepan to heat through or reheat in the microwave, stirring every minute, until hot.

Chicken and Cheese Soup

Stop! Best. Soup. Ever. We used Mersey Valley pickled onion cheese for this recipe – and it was positively amazing. OMG!

1 tablespoon olive oil

2 cloves garlic, crushed

½ bunch celery, diced

1 kg chicken thigh fillets, diced

4 cups chicken stock

250 g pickled onion cheese, crumbled

Heat the oil in large saucepan over high heat. Add the garlic, celery and chicken. Cook until the chicken has browned and the celery has started to go clear (about 5 minutes). Reduce the heat to medium and add the stock and cheese, stirring until the cheese starts to melt and blend into the stock. Reduce the heat to low and simmer for 45 minutes.

* *

Freezing: Allow to cool to room temperature then three-quarters fill a ziplock bag and store on a flat surface. Freeze for up to 3 months.

Thawing: Allow to sit in the fridge overnight.

Reheating: Place in a saucepan to heat through or reheat in the microwave, stirring every minute, until hot.

Hints & Tips

* Keep refrigerated for up to 3 days in an airtight container.

* If you don't have pickled onion cheese, add 2 chopped brown onions to the pan when browning the chicken and substitute grated tasty or sharp cheddar cheese for the pickled onion cheese.

Wonton Soup

This quick and easy Wonton Soup will take about 15 minutes to whip up and the next thing you know, it's time to eat! This soup will be pretty salty unless you ensure (where you can) that you use salt-reduced stock and soy sauce. Recipes that ask for ingredients to be julienned are simply using a fancy French word to describe very thin straws. You may have a kitchen whizzer that does that for you; alternatively, cut the ingredients as fine as you can with a sharp knife. Grating will also have a similar effect, but reduces the 'crunch' of the vegies.

1 litre salt-reduced chicken stock

1 litre water

3 cm piece ginger, peeled and julienned

1 clove garlic, crushed

30 frozen beef mini dim sims

¼ Chinese cabbage, shredded

2 carrots, peeled and julienned

½ cup salt-reduced soy sauce

1 cup bean sprouts

100 g snow peas, sliced lengthwise

4 spring onions, sliced

1 long red chilli, thinly sliced

coriander leaves, to serve

Place the stock, water, ginger and garlic into a saucepan over medium–high heat. Cover and bring to the boil. Reduce the heat to low, add the dim sims and simmer for 5 minutes or until the dim sims are cooked through. Add the cabbage, carrot and soy sauce. Stir to combine and simmer for 2–3 minutes, or until the vegetables are just tender. Remove the soup from the heat. Stir in the bean sprouts and snow peas. Ladle into serving bowls and top with spring onion, chilli and coriander.

Freezing: Allow to cool to room temperature then three-quarters fill a ziplock bag and store on a flat surface. Freeze for up to 6 months.

Thawing: Allow to sit in the fridge overnight.

Reheating: Place in a saucepan to heat through or reheat in the microwave, stirring every minute, until hot.

Cream of Broccoli Soup

A smooth, silky soup that is quick to prepare and tastes a treat; it'll soon be everyone's favourite.

1 cup raw cashews

2 cups chicken or vegetable stock

2 medium potatoes, peeled and quartered

1 brown onion, chopped

1 head broccoli, cut into florets

1 teaspoon chopped basil

celery salt

125 g cream cheese

Place the cashews and 1 cup of stock into a blender or food processor, and blend until smooth. Put the remaining stock, the potatoes and onion into a large saucepan and bring to the boil. Reduce the heat and simmer for 5 minutes before adding the broccoli and basil. Simmer until the potatoes are very tender, then stir in the cashew mixture and season with celery salt to taste. Remove from the heat and puree the soup in batches. Put back on the heat and stir in the cream cheese until the soup is hot and smooth.

* *

Freezing: Allow to cool to room temperature then three-quarters fill a ziplock bag and store on a flat surface. Freeze for up to 6 months.

Thawing: Allow to sit in the fridge overnight.

Reheating: Place in a saucepan to heat through or reheat in the microwave, stirring every minute, until hot.

Old-fashioned Cream of Mushroom Soup

If you love mushrooms and soup then this is definitely the meal for you!

1 tablespoon olive oil

1 onion, chopped

2 cloves garlic, crushed

750 g mushrooms, sliced

1½ tablespoons beef stock powder (use vegetable stock for a vegetarian version)

3 tablespoons Worcestershire sauce

3 tablespoons barbecue sauce

1 × 40 g packet French onion soup mix

2 litres water

4 tablespoons cornflour

1 × 375 ml can evaporated milk

Heat the oil in a large pot and sauté the onion and garlic for 2 minutes. Add the mushrooms, mix well and cook for 3 minutes. Add the stock powder, Worcestershire sauce, barbecue sauce, French onion soup mix and water to the pot and mix well. Bring to the boil then reduce the heat and simmer for 30 minutes. In a small bowl, combine the cornflour and evaporated milk then add to the pot while stirring; the mixture should thicken slightly.

* *

Freezing: Allow to cool to room temperature then three-quarters fill a ziplock bag and store on a flat surface. Freeze for up to 6 months.

Thawing: Allow to sit in the fridge overnight.

Reheating: Place in a saucepan to heat through or reheat in the microwave, stirring every minute, until hot.

Hints & Tips

* For a smoother soup, use a stick mixer or blender before serving.

Beef and Barley Soup

There is nothing quite like a cold winter's day huddled inside with something hearty and delicious that you know is going to hit the spot simmering in the slow cooker. This soup works especially well when served with cheesy toast.

1.5 kg gravy beef, cut into 1.5 cm pieces

1 cup barley

2 brown onions, chopped

1 green capsicum, roughly chopped

4 carrots, roughly chopped, skin left on

1 × 400 g can diced tomatoes

1 tablespoon tomato paste

1 litre beef stock

Add all ingredients to the slow cooker and stir well. Cook on high for 8 hours, stirring every so often. If the mixture resembles a casserole rather than a soup, add a bit more stock, but make sure it is still nice and thick and hearty!

* *

Freezing: Allow to cool to room temperature then three-quarters fill a ziplock bag and store on a flat surface. Freeze for up to 6 months.

Thawing: Allow to sit in the fridge overnight.

Reheating: Place in a saucepan to heat through or reheat in the microwave, stirring every minute, until hot.

Hints & Tips

* You can substitute lamb for the gravy beef.

Minestrone Soup

With some crusty buttered bread, this soup makes for a wholesome and delicious meal. It's nice and fast to prepare too – just what mums need!

1 tablespoon butter

1 large brown onion, finely chopped

1 clove garlic, crushed

2 rashers bacon, finely chopped (omit for vegetarian version)

1 stick celery, including leaves, chopped

1 carrot, peeled and chopped

1 x 410 g can crushed tomatoes

1 x 400 g can red kidney beans, drained and rinsed

3 cups beef stock (use vegetable stock for a vegetarian version)

1/3 cup penne or spiral pasta

1/2 cup grated parmesan cheese, to serve

2 tablespoons finely chopped fresh flat-leaf parsley, to serve

In a heavy-based saucepan over medium heat, melt the butter until bubbling. Add the onion, garlic and bacon. Stir until cooked (5–10 minutes). Add the celery and carrot and cook until caramelised. Stir in the tomato, kidney beans, beef stock and pasta. Simmer on low for 20–30 minutes or until the pasta is cooked through. Serve into bowls and top with the cheese and parsley.

* *

Freezing: Allow to cool to room temperature then three-quarters fill a ziplock bag and store on a flat surface. Freeze for up to 6 months.

Thawing: Allow to sit in the fridge overnight.

Reheating: Place in a saucepan to heat through or reheat in the microwave, stirring every minute, until hot.

Sausages

All girls love a good sausage. They are filling, and easily available. Try the honey-flavoured variety – good for everyday use!

Sausages in Pastry

I grew up eating Sausages in Pastry, and I make them for my family now. Sometimes I add a bit of cheese or sliced sweet potato for something different, but they always taste great and are a frugal choice. They don't last long in my house!

2 sheets puff pastry

8 sausages of your choice

mashed potato, to serve

steamed mixed vegetables, to serve

Preheat the oven to 180°C. Cut both sheets of pastry into quarters. Wrap a sausage in each piece of pastry diagonally. Place on a sheet of baking paper and bake in the oven for approximately 30 minutes, or until golden. Serve with mashed potato and mixed vegies.

* *

Freezing: Wrap uncooked in plastic wrap. Freeze for up to 4 months.

Thawing: Allow to sit in the fridge overnight.

Reheating: Cook as above.

Hints & Tips

* No need to pre-cook the sausages — they cook in the oven!

* For added flavour, try these variations:
- ~ a teaspoon of Dijon mustard
- ~ barbecue sauce and cheese
- ~ a slice of ham or bacon

Devilled Sausages

Devilled Sausages are one of my kids' favourite foods. They go really well with mashed potato and can be dressed up or down to be as hot or as mild as you like. We also have a great slow cooker version below.

6 beef or pork sausages

1 brown onion, diced

2 cloves garlic, crushed

¼ teaspoon curry powder (or to taste)

1 tablespoon caster sugar (or to taste)

1 × 410 g can crushed tomatoes

mashed potato, to serve

Brown the sausages in a frying pan. Remove and set aside. Add the onion to the pan and cook well. Add the garlic, curry powder, sugar and tomatoes and cook until reduced and thickened. Add the sausages to warm through and serve on mashed potato.

SLOW COOKER VERSION
Brown the sausages as above and place in the slow cooker. Add the remaining ingredients, except the mashed potato, and cook on high for 4 hours, stirring every hour or so.

* *

Freezing: Allow to cool then three-quarters fill a ziplock bag. Freeze for up to 4 months.

Thawing: Allow to sit in the fridge for up to 24 hours.

Reheating: Place in a saucepan to heat through or reheat in the microwave, stirring every minute, until hot.

Sausage Stroganoff

Looking for a new and different way to serve snags? Look no further.
Sausage Stroganoff works well with beef or pork sausages.

1 tablespoon olive oil

8 beef or pork
sausages, cut into
bite-sized pieces

2 cloves garlic, crushed

2 rashers bacon, finely
chopped

1 brown onion, finely
chopped

500 g mushrooms

2 tablespoons tomato
paste

1 teaspoon sweet
paprika

1 cup beef stock

½ cup sour cream

salt and pepper

pasta, to serve

Heat the olive oil in a heavy-based saucepan.
Add the sausages and cook until well browned
(about 10 minutes). Remove the sausages and
keep warm. Add the garlic, bacon, onion and
mushrooms to the pan and cook until browned
and soft. Add the tomato paste, paprika and beef
stock. Simmer gently for a few minutes. Return
the sausages to the pan and heat through. Turn
off the heat and stir in the sour cream. Season
with salt and pepper to taste. Serve over hot pasta.

* *

Freezing: Allow to cool then three-quarters
fill a ziplock bag. Freeze for up to 4 months.
(Don't add the sour cream before freezing as
it might curdle.)

Thawing: Allow to sit in the fridge for up to 24 hours.

Reheating: Place in a saucepan to heat through
or reheat in the microwave, stirring every minute,
until hot.

Slow Cooker Sausages in Onion Gravy

Slow Cooker Sausages in Onion Gravy is a great idea for big or small family dinners, as it's so simple to make. It will probably become an old favourite in your family. Serve with either mashed potato or crusty bread.

1 large brown onion, sliced into thin rings

8 sausages, either whole or chopped into bite-sized pieces

2 tablespoons gravy mix

1 clove garlic, crushed

Place the onion rings in the bottom of the slow cooker and arrange the sausages on top. Combine the gravy mix, garlic and 2 cups of hot water in a jug. Pour over the sausages. Cook on low for 4 hours.

* *

Freezing: Allow to cool then three-quarters fill a ziplock bag. Freeze for up to 4 months.

Thawing: Allow to sit in the fridge for up to 24 hours.

Reheating: Place in a saucepan to heat through or reheat in the microwave, stirring every minute, until hot.

Hints & Tips

* If you have any fresh herbs on hand, throw them in when you add the gravy mix.

Sausage Casserole

Sausage Casserole is an easy 'all in' recipe – a great dinner for the family!

2 medium potatoes, thinly sliced

2 carrots, sliced

1 large brown onion, sliced

¼ cup rice

6–8 thick sausages

1 × 420 g can tomato soup

½ can water (use the tomato soup can as a measure)

1 cup grated tasty cheese

Preheat the oven to 180°C. Layer the potato into the base of a casserole dish then add a layer of carrot. Separate the onion rings and layer on top of the carrot. Sprinkle the rice over then arrange the sausages on top. Pour in the tomato soup and water. Cover and bake for 1½ hours. Remove the lid and cook for another 30 minutes, sprinkling the cheese over the top 15 minutes from the end.

* *

Freezing: Allow to cool then cut into serving portions. Place into an aluminium container and cover with the cardboard lid. Freeze for up to 6 months.

Thawing: Allow to sit in the fridge for up to 24 hours.

Reheating: Place the aluminium container in a preheated oven at 180°C for 20 minutes. Remove the lid for the last 10 minutes to brown.

Coconut Curry Sausage Casserole

Creamy, meaty deliciousness. A lovely meal to come home to when there is a chill in the air.

500 g pork sausages (chopped or whole, as you prefer)

1 small brown onion, finely diced

500 g chopped fresh vegetables (I use choko, pumpkin, potato, carrot – pretty much whatever I have extra of)

2 tablespoons mild curry powder

1 clove garlic, crushed

1 × 400 ml can coconut cream

Place the sausages, onion and vegetables into a slow cooker. Mix the curry powder, garlic and coconut cream together. Pour over the sausages and mix well. Cook on low for 6 hours.

* *

Freezing: Allow to cool then three-quarters fill a ziplock bag. Freeze for up to 4 months.

Thawing: Allow to sit in the fridge for up to 24 hours.

Reheating: Place in a saucepan to heat through or reheat in the microwave, stirring every minute, until hot.

Curried Sausages

One of our fabulous SAHMs, Clancy, was searching for a simple recipe for Curried Sausages that she could whip up in a minute and that would be eaten just as quick. One call to her mum gave her this super simple, frugal recipe. It went down a treat.

500 g sausages (beef, pork or chicken – the choice is yours!)

1 brown onion, chopped

curry powder

1 tablespoon cornflour

¾ cup water

rice, to serve

pappadams, to serve

You don't need to cook the sausages beforehand, but I cook mine in a saucepan for 5 minutes just to seal the meat and then chop them into 5 cm pieces. Place the sausages and onion into a large saucepan and cover with water. Place over low–medium heat. Add curry powder to taste (I use 2 tablespoons) and leave to simmer until your sausages are cooked through. In a small bowl, combine the cornflour and water to make a smooth paste and add to the curry. Turn up the heat and cook until the sauce thickens. Serve with rice and pappadams.

Freezing: Allow to cool then three-quarters fill a ziplock bag. Freeze for up to 4 months.

Thawing: Allow to sit in the fridge for up to 24 hours.

Reheating: Place in a saucepan to heat through or reheat in the microwave, stirring every minute, until hot.

Hints & Tips

* You can add fruit, such as sultanas and apples, if you like your curry with a fruity kick.

* Carrots and peas can also bulk up this meal and add to your daily vegie intake.

* This recipe can be made in the slow cooker – just add uncooked sausages and cut up midway through cooking. Takes about 4 hours on low.

* For a different flavour, replace the water with a can of coconut cream.

For other simple, frugal recipes see:

* Rustic Tomato Soup – page 49

* Homemade Chicken Nuggets – page 93

* Chickpea Curry – page 114

* Pasta and Pesto – page 120

Mince

Mince is the ultimate frugal meal. I like to shop on Saturday afternoons when most of the supermarkets have meat on sale. I buy the mince in 500 g packs and freeze them as is – if you have mince in the freezer, you always have a meal on hand.

Bulk Bolognaise Sauce

Bulk Bolognaise Sauce is a great way to save time and money in the kitchen, as it is a family favourite and so versatile.

2 brown onions, finely chopped

4 cloves garlic, finely chopped

2 carrots, diced

2 sticks celery, diced

2 kg mince

2 × 410 g cans crushed tomatoes

1 × 420 g can tomato soup

Place the onion and garlic in a slow cooker. Cook for approximately 30 minutes on high to allow them to heat through and soften. Add the carrot, celery and mince and cook for a further hour, stirring well every so often. Pour in the tomatoes and soup and cook on low for 6 hours.

* *

Freezing: Allow to cool then three-quarters fill a ziplock bag. Freeze for up to 6 months.

Thawing: Allow to sit in the fridge for up to 24 hours.

Reheating: Place in a saucepan to heat through or reheat in the microwave, stirring every minute, until hot.

Hints & Tips

* Apart from serving on pasta, you could heap the bolognaise onto jacket potatoes with sour cream and cheese, serve it on nachos or in tacos. Omit the tomato soup and you have savoury mince that can be served on toast or topped with potato for a shepherd's pie!

Savoury Mince

Savoury Mince is always a good stand-by for a quick meal. It can be used as a main dish with rice or pasta, a filling for pastries or on toast – the list is endless!

2 tablespoons olive oil

1 brown onion, finely chopped

2 cloves garlic, crushed

600 g beef mince

1 teaspoon beef stock powder

any extra spices or flavours you wish to add e.g. curry spices, chillies, herbs etc.

1 large carrot, peeled and finely chopped

any extra vegies you wish to add e.g. peas, beans, corn, etc.

2 tablespoons tomato paste

2 × 410 g cans crushed tomatoes

splash of Worcestershire sauce

salt and pepper

Heat the oil in a large saucepan over medium heat. Add the onion and garlic and cook, stirring, for 5 minutes, or until the onion is soft. Add the mince, beef stock powder and any spices you like. Cook, stirring occasionally, until the mince has browned. Add the carrot and any other vegies. Cook, stirring, for another 5 minutes. Add the tomato paste and stir for 2 minutes. Add the tomatoes and Worcestershire sauce. Increase the heat to bring to the boil. Once boiling, reduce the heat to medium–low and simmer, uncovered, for 20–30 minutes, until the sauce thickens. Season with salt and pepper to taste.

* *

Freezing: Allow to cool then three-quarters fill a ziplock bag. Freeze for up to 6 months.

Thawing: Allow to sit in the fridge for up to 24 hours.

Reheating: Place in a saucepan to heat through or reheat in the microwave, stirring every minute, until hot.

Gassy Lasagne

Yes, you read that right. Gassy Lasagne has a certain reputation not only for being delicious but also for making people – ahem – fart. I'm not sure what it is about my recipe that does this but it has become a bit of a joke among my friends now. Don't worry, though, it's a very mild side effect!

canola oil spray

2 teaspoons olive oil

1 brown onion, finely diced

2 cloves garlic, crushed

1 kg beef mince

1 beef stock cube

2 × 410 g cans crushed tomatoes

1 × 420 g can tomato soup

2 packets lasagne sheets

Preheat the oven to 180°C. Lightly spray a large baking or ceramic dish with canola oil. Heat the olive oil in a large saucepan over medium heat. Fry off the onion and garlic until fragrant. Add the mince and brown well. Crumble the beef stock cube into the mince and stir well. Add the tomatoes and the soup. Reduce the heat to low, cover, and simmer for about 20 minutes so the mixture reduces and thickens. Leave the lid on and set aside to cool slightly. Make the cheese sauce (see opposite). Start layering the bolognaise sauce, lasagne sheets (don't overlap them) and then the cheese sauce on top. Keep layering until the mixture is all used up but try and finish on the cheese sauce layer. Add the remaining cup of grated cheese and bake in the oven for 40 minutes until golden and the lasagne sheets are cooked through.

CHEESE SAUCE

3 tablespoons butter

3 tablespoons plain flour

500 ml milk

2 chicken stock cubes

3 cups grated cheddar cheese

Place the butter in a microwave-safe jug and microwave on high for about 30 seconds, or until bubbling. Add the flour and mix well. Buzz for another 20–30 seconds to 'cook out the flour' (this will ensure your white sauce does not have a floury taste yet still has a thick consistency). Whisking continuously, slowly add the milk, making sure there are no lumps. Crumble the chicken stock cubes into the sauce and add 2 cups of the grated cheese. Microwave in 30-second increments, whisking well between each blast, until the cheese has melted and the sauce is smooth.

* *

Freezing: Place in an aluminium foil container (or freezer-to-oven container) and cover in plastic wrap. Freeze for up to 4 months.

Thawing: Allow to sit in the fridge for up to 48 hours.

Reheating: Place a lid on the container and place in a preheated oven at 180°C for 20 minutes, or until heated through. Remove the lid for the last 10 minutes to brown.

Chilli Con Carne

Chilli Con Carne is great in tacos or burritos, on toast or on its own – however you like to serve it, it's delish.

1 tablespoon olive oil

1 large brown onion, diced

1 clove garlic, crushed

500 g mince

1 × 420 g can tomato soup

1 teaspoon hot chilli sauce

salt and pepper

1 × 125 g can red kidney beans

sour cream, to serve (optional)

grated cheddar cheese, to serve (optional)

Heat the olive oil in a saucepan and fry the onion, garlic and mince until the meat is well browned. Add the tomato soup and chilli sauce. Season with salt and pepper to taste. Simmer gently for 15–20 minutes or until thickened. Add the undrained kidney beans and heat through. Serve topped with a dollop of sour cream and a sprinkling of grated cheese, if desired.

* *

Freezing: Allow to cool then three-quarters fill a ziplock bag. Freeze for up to 8 months.

Thawing: Allow to sit in the fridge for up to 24 hours.

Reheating: Place in a saucepan to heat through.

Beef Chow Mein

This delicious recipe keeps all the taste of traditional chow mein, but in a budget version. I tend to serve it as is, but you could also have it on toast or in a lettuce cup.

1 tablespoon olive oil

1 onion, chopped

1 clove garlic, crushed

500 g beef mince

1 cup mixed frozen vegetables

2 cups cabbage (optional)

1 small packet rice noodles or two-minute noodles

2–3 teaspoons curry powder (depending on taste)

Heat the oil in a frying pan over medium heat. Fry the onion and garlic until starting to brown, then add the mince and brown well. Add the vegetables and cabbage, if using. Put a lid on the pan and cook for 5 minutes, or until the vegies are tender. Meanwhile, boil the kettle and prepare the noodles according to the packet instructions, except slightly under-cook them. Add the curry powder to the mince mixture one teaspoon at a time until you like the taste (the more you add, the tastier it is – but kids might not like it too hot). Stir through the noodles.

Freezing: Allow to cool to room temperature then three-quarters fill a ziplock bag. Freeze for up to 3 months.

Thawing: Allow to sit in the fridge overnight.

Reheating: Place in a frying pan to heat through.

Mince Wellington

Mince Wellington is an inexpensive dish that the kids will adore. Like a cross between a big sausage roll and a meatloaf, it looks and tastes great.

500 g lean beef mince

1 tablespoon milk

2 teaspoons Tuscan seasoning or mixed herbs

2 tablespoons tomato sauce

¾ cup breadcrumbs

1 tablespoon oil

1 onion, diced

2 cloves garlic, crushed

125 g mushrooms, sliced

2 sheets puff pastry

1 egg, beaten

Preheat the oven to 190°C. Line a baking tray with baking paper. Place the mince, milk, seasoning, tomato sauce and breadcrumbs into a large bowl. Mix with a wooden spoon or your hands to combine well. Heat the oil in a frying pan and add the onion, garlic and mushrooms. Cook until the onion is clear and the mushrooms have browned. Drain off any juices and place on paper towel to drain further (this prevents the pastry from going soggy). Lay the pastry sheets on the baking tray, overlapping along one long edge by 1 centimetre. Press down with your fingers to join the pastry along this seam. Place half of the mushroom mixture along the centre of the pastry sheets in a wide line, leaving 5 centimetres at either end. Top with the mince mixture, forming a log shape. Top with the remaining mushroom mixture. Wrap up doing the sides first then tucking the ends under as you turn it over. Prick the top with a fork and brush with beaten egg. Bake for 40 minutes, or until the pastry is golden.

Hints & Tips

* For an even healthier version, add some grated zucchini, carrot, peas and corn.

* Keep refrigerated in an airtight container for up to 4 days.

Freezing: Allow to cool to room temperature then wrap in aluminium foil, then in plastic wrap. Freeze for up to 2 months.

Thawing: Allow to sit in the fridge overnight or on the kitchen counter for up to an hour.

Reheating: Place in a preheated oven at 190°C for 20 minutes, or until hot.

Hamburgers

These patties are simple to make and freeze really well, so you can always have hamburgers on the table in just a few minutes. Perfect for after-school activities!

300 g beef mince

1 egg

20 g French onion soup mix

½ onion, finely diced

1 tablespoon tomato sauce

¾ cup breadcrumbs

2 tablespoons milk

1 tablespoon olive oil

6 hamburger buns

6 cheese slices

mayonnaise, for spreading

½ iceberg lettuce, shredded

2 tomatoes, sliced

6 beetroot slices

6 pineapple rings

barbecue sauce, for spreading

Place the mince, egg, soup mix, onion, tomato sauce, breadcrumbs and milk in a bowl and mix with your hands until well combined. Roll into six hamburger patties. Heat the olive oil in a frying pan over medium–high heat. Add the patties and cook for 4–5 minutes each side, until browned and cooked through. Halve the hamburger buns. Place a slice of cheese on half the bun halves, then place under the grill until the cheese melts. Spread mayonnaise on the other side of the buns and top with lettuce, tomato, beetroot and a pineapple ring. Place a patty on top and a dollop of barbecue sauce. Place the cheesy toasted bun halves on top and serve.

Freezing: Allow patties to cool to room temperature then place on baking paper and seal in an airtight container or ziplock bag. Freeze for up to 1 month.

Thawing: Allow to sit in the fridge overnight or on the kitchen counter for up to an hour.

Reheating: Pan fry until heated through.

Beef and Macaroni Bake

Easy to make and easy on the pocket – a great way to fill up hungry tummies.

1 tablespoon olive oil

1 brown onion, finely diced

1 clove garlic, crushed

500 g beef mince

1 tablespoon Worcestershire sauce

2 teaspoons dried mixed herbs

2 × 410 g tins crushed tomatoes

2 cups uncooked macaroni noodles

1½ cups grated cheese

OPTIONAL TOPPING

½ punnet cherry tomatoes

12 basil leaves

3 sprigs rosemary

Preheat the oven to 180°C. Heat the oil in a frying pan over medium heat. Fry the onion and garlic until soft. Add the mince and brown well. Add the Worcestershire sauce, herbs and tomatoes. Reduce the heat and simmer for 10 minutes, or until slightly thickened. Meanwhile, boil the noodles in a large pot of salted boiling water until just tender. Drain well. Spoon half the mince mixture into the base of a large baking dish, then top with the noodles. Place the remaining mince mixture on top. Sprinkle with grated cheese and bake for 15 minutes, or until the cheese is starting to brown. For an additional taste sensation, sprinkle the cheese on top then add the cherry tomatoes, basil and rosemary and press gently into the cheese before baking.

Freezing: Place in an aluminium container (or freezer-to-oven container) and cover in plastic wrap. Freeze for up to 3 months.

Thawing: Allow to sit in the fridge for up to 24 hours.

Reheating: Place a lid on the container and place in a preheated oven at 180°C for 20 minutes, or until heated through. Take the lid off for the last 10 minutes to brown.

Hints & Tips

* You can substitute pork, turkey or chicken mince for the beef.
* Keep covered in the fridge for up to 4 days.

Porcupine Mince Balls

Porcupine Mince Balls are like a bulked-up spaghetti bolognaise recipe, and are a firm family favourite! Just make sure you have enough liquid, so your rice doesn't go crunchy.

500 g beef mince

1 egg

1 brown onion, diced

½ cup long-grain rice

1 clove garlic, crushed

1 × 420 g can tomato soup

Preheat the oven to 180°C. Mix all the ingredients, except for the tomato soup, together in a bowl. Roll dessertspoonfuls of the mixture into balls and place in a pie dish. Place the tomato soup into a microwave-proof bowl with 1 cup of water. Microwave until hot. Stir well and pour over the meatballs. Bake for 30 minutes, or until cooked through.

Freezing: Allow to cool to room temperature then three-quarters fill a ziplock bag. Freeze for up to 3 months.

Thawing: Allow to sit in the fridge overnight.

Reheating: Pour into an ovenproof container and place in a preheated oven at 180°C for 10 minutes.

Hints & Tips

* The rice needs to be uncooked. If it appears the rice is still crunchy when baking, it means there isn't enough liquid for the rice to 'suck up'. Add a bit more soup or water.
* Chicken mince can be substituted for the beef mince.
* You can also add a tablespoon of dried mixed herbs, a teaspoon of sugar and ½ cup of breadcrumbs for a different version. If adding the breadcrumbs, bake for about 45 minutes.

Potato Gem Casserole

If your kids are anything like mine, they love potato gems. Tater tots, potato royals, whatever you call them, these little balls of fluffy mash with a crispy golden coating are not only cheap but also fantastically versatile. Try them in this casserole.

500 g beef mince

1 brown onion, roughly chopped

1 × 420 g can cream of mushroom soup

1 tablespoon tomato ketchup (NOT tomato sauce!)

1 tablespoon Worcestershire sauce

3 cups potato gems

Preheat the oven to 220°C. In a large frying pan, cook the mince and onion, breaking up any lumps, until the mince is well browned. Add the soup, ketchup and Worcestershire sauce and stir to combine. Spoon into a 2-litre baking dish. Arrange the potato gems around the edges of the baking dish, leaving some of the mince mixture exposed in the middle. Bake for 25–30 minutes, or until the potato gems are golden.

* *

Freezing: Place in an aluminium foil container (or freezer-to-oven container) and cover in plastic wrap. Freeze for up to 3 months.

Thawing: Allow to sit in the fridge for up to 24 hours.

Reheating: Place a lid on the container and place in a preheated oven at 180°C for 20 minutes, or until heated through. Take the lid off for the last 10 minutes to brown.

Shepherd's Pie Cupcakes

Tired of doing shepherd's pie the traditional way? The whole family will love Shepherd's Pie Cupcakes with their yummy sweet potato topping.

3 large sweet potatoes, peeled and diced

2 teaspoons butter

1 tablespoon Tuscan seasoning

2 teaspoons oil

1 onion, diced

1 clove garlic, crushed

600 g beef mince

1 tablespoon gravy mix

1 tablespoon Worcestershire sauce

Preheat the oven to 180°C. Line a 12-hole muffin tin with paper cases. Bring 2 cups of water to the boil in a medium saucepan. Add the sweet potato and boil for 5 minutes, then reduce the heat and simmer until the potato is soft when tested with a fork. Drain then place the potatoes back in the saucepan and add the butter and Tuscan seasoning. Mash with a potato masher until smooth. Heat the oil in a frying pan over medium heat. Fry the onion and garlic until the onion is clear. Add the mince and cook until well browned. Stir in the gravy mix and Worcestershire sauce. Divide the mixture between the holes in the muffin tin. Top with the sweet potato mixture. Bake for 15 minutes, or until crunchy and golden.

Freezing: Place into an airtight container lined with baking paper and cover loosely with baking paper. Freeze for up to 1 month.

Thawing: Reheat from frozen.

Reheating: Place in a preheated oven at 200°C for 15 minutes, or until crunchy and golden.

Hints & Tips

* Potato, pumpkin or a combination of the two can be substituted for the sweet potato.

Chicken

Chicken would probably have to be one of my very favourite meats. It is so versatile and is loved by all the family. If you were only going to make one recipe, try my Chicken Pot Pie. It is delicious any time of year, freezes beautifully and you can add so many vegetables to the mix that it truly is a whole meal in one.

Chicken Stock

Chicken stock is probably the most versatile homemade stock to make. It is the base for many soups and is a great way to add flavour to cooked rice or quinoa. You can also make chicken stock into a sauce or gravy, boiling to reduce by half and then thickening with cornflour and seasoning well. The secret to a really tasty chicken stock is to bake your chicken carcass in the oven on a very high heat for 15 minutes before making the stock. You don't strictly need to do this step – but it does make for a tastier result!

chicken carcasses

vegetables (onions, celery, carrots – whatever you have on hand)

Place the chicken carcasses and a heap of vegetables into a large saucepan and cover with water. Boil for approximately 4 hours (or cook in the slow cooker on high for 8 hours), skimming the 'scum' off the top every so often and discarding. Allow the stock to cool a little then strain well. Let the stock cool to room temperature before placing in the fridge for up to 7 days. This allows any fat to rise to the top which can then be scooped off and discarded.

Freezing: Pour the stock into ice cube containers. Allow to freeze solid then remove and place in a ziplock bag. Freeze for up to 6 months.

Thawing: Don't thaw, add frozen as required.

Reheating: Place in a microwave-proof container or a saucepan and heat until hot.

Hints & Tips

* If you buy a whole chicken from a takeaway store, you can use this carcass to make stock. So don't throw it out – freeze it!

Gooey Cheesy Chicken Rissoles

These rissoles ooze cheese when you cut into them, then melt in your mouth. Life just got a whole lot better.

500 g chicken mince

1 onion, finely chopped

1 egg, beaten

2 tablespoons breadcrumbs

150 g extra sharp or tasty cheese, cut into 10 cubes

1 tablespoon olive oil

Place the mince, onion, egg and breadcrumbs in a bowl and mix with your fingers until well combined. Shape into 10 balls and press a cube of cheese into each rissole. Roll again to ensure the cheese is in the centre. Heat the oil in a frying pan over medium–high heat and cook the rissoles for 3–5 minutes each side. They will turn white on the edge and golden brown on each side when cooked.

Freezing: Allow to cool to room temperature then place on baking paper and seal in an airtight container or ziplock bag. Freeze for up to 1 month.

Thawing: Allow to sit in the fridge overnight or on the kitchen counter for up to an hour.

Reheating: Pan fry until heated through.

Hints & Tips

* Serve with a fresh garden salad.

Chicken Cordon Bleu Casserole

Chicken with cheese and ham – doesn't get much better than that!

1 egg

1½ cups milk

1 kg chicken pieces

100 g breadcrumbs

⅓ cup olive oil

250 g ham, chopped

200 g tasty cheese, cubed

1 × 420 g can cream of chicken soup

Preheat the oven to 180°C. Beat the egg and half a cup of the milk together in a large bowl until combined. Add the chicken and coat with the mixture, then drain. Place the breadcrumbs on a plate and roll the chicken in them to coat. Heat the oil in a heavy frying pan and fry the chicken in batches until golden on all sides. Remove and drain on paper towel. Place the chicken in a baking dish. Sprinkle the ham and cheese over the top. Stir together the soup and the remaining milk and pour over the top. Bake for 30 minutes, or until golden brown and bubbling.

Freezing: Place in an aluminium foil container (or freezer-to-oven container) and cover with plastic wrap. Freeze for up to 3 months.

Thawing: Allow to sit in the fridge for up to 48 hours.

Reheating: Place a lid on the baking dish or container and reheat in the oven at 180°C for 20 minutes, or until heated through.

Chicken Casserole with Cheesy Damper Top

This is a creamy, delicious meal that the whole family will enjoy! Good all year round, serve with steamed vegetables in winter and a fresh salad and crusty bread in the warmer months.

40 g butter

3 chicken breast fillets, cut into 2 cm pieces

1 onion, chopped

250 g bacon, diced

1 × 420 g can cream of chicken soup

300 ml sour cream

DAMPER TOP

1 cup self-raising flour

2 eggs

2 cups grated tasty cheese

½ cup milk

Preheat the oven to 180°C. Heat the butter in a frying pan until it melts then lightly brown the chicken pieces. Add the onion and bacon to the pan and cook for 2–3 minutes, or until fragrant and the onion has softened. Pour in the soup and add the sour cream. Mix until well combined. Pour the mixture into a pie dish and set aside. To make the damper top, sift the flour into a bowl. Add the eggs, 1½ cups of the cheese and the milk. Mix until just blended. Pour the damper top batter over the casserole and bake uncovered for 30 minutes. Sprinkle with the remaining cheese and bake a further 5 minutes.

* *

Freezing: Place in an aluminium foil container (or freezer-to-oven container) and cover with plastic wrap. Freeze for up to 3 months.

Thawing: Allow to sit in the fridge for up to 24 hours.

Reheating: Place a lid on the pie dish or container and reheat in the oven at 180°C for 20 minutes.

Hints & Tips

* For more vegetable content, steam a cup of vegetables such as broccoli, corn and peas, and add to the mixture just before adding the damper top.

Mustard Chicken Casserole

Mustard Chicken Casserole combines a lot of flavours to come up with a beautiful dish that the whole family can enjoy. It can be served with rice, mashed potato or pasta.

3 carrots, sliced into rounds

1 head broccoli, cut into small florets

2 chicken breasts, sliced in half lengthwise

salt and pepper

1 tablespoon olive oil

1 × 420 g can cream of chicken soup

1 can milk (measured using the soup can)

2 teaspoons wholegrain mustard

½ cup grated tasty cheese

Preheat the oven to 180°C. Layer the vegies in the bottom of an ovenproof and microwave-safe dish, cover loosely with plastic wrap and zap in the microwave for 2–3 minutes, or until just tender. Season the chicken with salt and pepper. Heat the oil in a frying pan over medium–high heat and cook the chicken for 1 minute each side, or until just browned. (You could skip the browning step if really pushed for time.) Place the chicken breasts evenly over the vegies in one layer. In a jug, whisk together the soup, milk and mustard. Pour the soup mixture evenly over the chicken and vegies. Top with grated cheese and bake for 20–30 minutes, or until golden and bubbling.

Freezing: Place in an aluminium foil container (or freezer-to-oven container) and cover with plastic wrap. Freeze for up to 3 months.

Thawing: Allow to sit in the fridge for up to 24 hours.

Reheating: Place a lid on the dish or container and reheat in the oven at 180°C for 20 minutes. Take the lid off for the last 10 minutes to brown.

Chicken and Mushroom Bake

Chicken and Mushroom Bake is one of our simplest and yet tastiest dishes. Easy-peasy to make and everyone will love it!

1 × 420 g can cream of mushroom soup

⅓ cup milk

8 chicken drumsticks

garlic salt

ground paprika

Preheat the oven to 170°C. Mix the soup and milk together in a medium bowl or jug. Place the chicken drumsticks in a medium baking dish and lightly coat with garlic salt. Pour the soup mixture over the top and sprinkle the chicken with paprika. Bake for 90 minutes uncovered in the oven.

Freezing: Place in an aluminium foil container (or freezer-to-oven container) and cover in plastic wrap and seal well. Freeze for up to 3 months.

Thawing: Allow to sit in the fridge for up to 48 hours.

Reheating: Place a lid on the baking dish or container and reheat in the oven at 180°C for 20 minutes, or until heated through.

Chicken Pot Pie

Chicken Pot Pie is a staple meal in my house. Try it with mashed potato or on rice.

1 teaspoon olive oil

1 brown onion, finely diced

2 cloves garlic, crushed

200 g bacon rashers, finely chopped

2 chicken breasts, diced

1 cup frozen vegetables

1 × 375 ml can evaporated milk

¾ cup grated cheddar cheese

salt and pepper

1 tablespoon cornflour

1 sheet puff pastry

garden salad, to serve

Preheat the oven to 200°C. Heat the oil in a heavy-based saucepan. Fry the onion, garlic and bacon until cooked through. Add the chicken and cook for 3–4 minutes, or until cooked through. Stir in the vegetables, milk and cheese. Cook for 5–7 minutes, stirring often, until the vegetables are tender. Season with salt and pepper to taste. Mix the cornflour with a tablespoon of warm water to make a paste. Keep adding warm water until the mixture is the consistency of thick soup. Stir into the chicken mixture. Pour into a pie dish and place the puff pastry over the top, trimming the edges. Bake for 20 minutes or until the puff pastry is golden. Serve with a garden salad.

* *

Freezing: Allow the chicken mixture (minus the pastry) to cool to room temperature then three-quarters fill a ziplock bag and lay flat in the freezer. Freeze for up to 4 months.

Thawing: Allow to sit in the fridge overnight.

Reheating: Place into a pie dish, top with puff pastry and cook until the pastry is golden and the chicken mixture is hot.

Hints & Tips

* Chicken mince (approximately 500 grams) can be used instead of chicken breasts.

Slow Cooker Curried Chicken

This curried chicken recipe is great because you can chuck it in the slow cooker and just leave it for a few hours. The result tastes super delicious!

3 large chicken breasts, cut into 1.5 cm chunks

½ cup chicken stock

1 × 420 g can cream of chicken soup

1 brown onion, chopped

1 red capsicum, finely chopped

200 g baby spinach (optional)

1½ teaspoons curry powder

¼ teaspoon ground ginger

noodles or rice, to serve

Place the chicken into the slow cooker. Combine the rest of the ingredients and pour over the top. Cover and cook on low for 4 hours. Serve on noodles or rice.

* *

Freezing: Allow to cool to room temperature then three-quarters fill a ziplock bag and lay flat in the freezer. Freeze for up to 4 months.

Thawing: Allow to sit in the fridge overnight.

Reheating: Reheat in the microwave or a saucepan until heated through.

Hints & Tips

* For an even richer version, add a can of coconut cream.

Chicken Peanut Curry

This Chicken Peanut Curry can be as hot or mild as you wish – but it's sure to warm you up on a cold winter's night!

8 chicken thighs

¼ cup olive oil

2 tablespoons red curry paste

1 × 400 ml can coconut milk

¼ cup fish sauce

2 tablespoons brown sugar

½ cup crunchy peanut butter

jasmine rice, to serve

Asian greens, to serve

Preheat the oven to 190°C. Place the chicken pieces on a baking tray and brush with half the olive oil. Bake for 40 minutes, or until cooked through. In a heavy-based saucepan, heat the remaining oil and fry off the curry paste. Stir in the coconut milk, fish sauce, sugar and peanut butter. Stir over medium heat until the mixture boils and thickens slightly. Add the chicken and heat through. Serve on jasmine rice with steamed Asian greens.

* *

Freezing: Allow to cool to room temperature then three-quarters fill a ziplock bag and lay flat in the freezer. Freeze for up to 4 months.

Thawing: Allow to sit in the fridge overnight.

Reheating: Reheat in the microwave or a saucepan until heated through.

Chicken Kiev

Chicken Kiev patties – they don't cost a fortune and are so easy to make!

500 g chicken breast, roughly chopped

2 cloves garlic, crushed

½ cup flavoured cream cheese (such as onion and chive)

20 g parmesan cheese, grated

¼ cup chopped fresh flat-leaf parsley

1 cup plain flour

2 eggs, beaten

2 cups breadcrumbs

Preheat the oven to 200°C. Combine the chicken, garlic, cream cheese, parmesan and parsley in a food processor and process until smooth. Form into eight patties. Roll the patties in flour, then in the egg, then in the breadcrumbs. Place on a baking tray and bake for 20–25 minutes, or until lightly browned and crisp.

* *

Freezing: Allow to cool to room temperature then wrap in aluminium foil, then in plastic wrap. Freeze for up to 2 months.

Thawing: Allow to sit in the fridge overnight or on the kitchen counter for up to an hour.

Reheating: Place in a preheated oven at 180°C for 10 minutes, or until hot.

Chicken Wellingtons

Chicken Wellingtons are easy and fun to make, so are great for the kids to help with. These chicken pockets are also perfect for entertaining – either as a main or a starter, as they can be made any size.

1 tablespoon butter

4 spring onions, finely chopped

1 cup sliced mushrooms

2 sheets puff pastry

4 small chicken breasts (or 2 large cut in half lengthwise)

4 tablespoons made up chicken gravy

1 egg, beaten

salad leaves, to serve

Preheat the oven to 200°C. Line a baking tray with baking paper. Melt the butter in a saucepan over medium heat and add the spring onions and mushrooms. Cook for 3 minutes then set aside to cool. Cut each pastry sheet in half. Place a quarter of the mushroom mixture on the centre of each piece of pastry. Place a chicken breast on top of the mushroom mixture. Spread the top of the chicken with the gravy. Fold the pastry up over the chicken, tucking the ends under to seal. Glaze with the beaten egg. Bake for 30–35 minutes, until golden. Serve with a lovely fresh salad.

* *

Freezing: Allow to cool to room temperature then double wrap in plastic wrap. Freeze for up to 6 months.

Thawing: Allow to sit in the fridge overnight.

Reheating: Place in a preheated oven at 180°C for 10 minutes, or until the centre is piping hot.

Homemade Chicken Nuggets

Homemade Chicken Nuggets are a healthy alternative to the takeaway version. This way you know that what you have put into them is actually chicken!

1 egg

1 tablespoon milk

1 cup crushed corn flakes

¼ cup finely grated parmesan cheese

500 g chicken thigh fillets, cut into 3 cm pieces

¼ cup plain flour

canola oil spray

Preheat the oven to 180°C. Line a baking tray with baking paper. Combine the egg and milk in a bowl. Combine the corn flakes and cheese in another bowl. Coat the chicken pieces in flour, dip in the combined egg and milk mixture then roll in the corn-flake mixture until coated well. Place on the baking tray, spray with canola oil and bake for 25 minutes, or until lightly browned and cooked through.

＊ ＊

Freezing: Cook the nuggets until the batter is sealed only (about 1 minute). Allow the half-cooked nuggets to cool to room temperature. Wrap in baking paper or paper towel to absorb the oil, then wrap in plastic wrap. Freeze for up to 2 months.

Thawing: Do not need to be thawed, cook from frozen.

Reheating: Place in a preheated oven at 180°C for 10 minutes, or until hot, or deep fry until golden.

Chicken Filo Parcels

This is a great 'make in advance' chicken recipe – perfect for freezer cooking!

4 sheets filo pastry

2 teaspoons butter

2 tablespoons olive oil

1 carrot, julienned

2 spring onions, sliced into strips

75 g Chinese cabbage, thinly sliced

2 tablespoons breadcrumbs

2 teaspoons chopped thyme leaves

2 teaspoons chopped sage

50 g smoked ham, chopped

½ small brown onion, diced

250 g chicken mince

1 teaspoon sesame seeds

Preheat the oven to 190°C. Cut each sheet of filo pastry in half lengthwise to make rectangles. Melt the butter then mix it with the olive oil. Blanch the carrot, spring onion and cabbage by placing in boiling water for 1 minute. Drain then drop the vegies into a bowl of cold water for a moment. Pat dry with paper towel and place in a large mixing bowl. Add the breadcrumbs, herbs, ham, brown onion and chicken mince. Mix well. Brush a filo pastry strip with the oil and butter mixture and then place one eighth of the chicken filling on one short edge. Roll up the pastry with the filling inside, crimping in the outside edges as you go so that it resembles a spring roll. Place on a baking tray and brush with more of the oil and butter mixture. Repeat for the rest of the parcels. Use a fork to score some slices diagonally on the top of each parcel, sprinkle on some sesame seeds, and place in the oven until the pastry turns golden (about 30 minutes). While the parcels are cooking, make the cranberry relish (see opposite). Serve the parcels with the relish alongside.

Freezing: Allow the cooked parcels to cool to room temperature. Wrap in aluminium foil, then wrap in plastic wrap. Freeze for up to 2 months.

Thawing: Allow to sit in the fridge overnight or on the kitchen counter for up to an hour.

Reheating: Place in a preheated oven at 180°C for 10 minutes, or until hot.

CRANBERRY RELISH

2 teaspoons olive oil

1 teaspoon English mustard

¼ cup cranberry sauce

1 tablespoon red-wine vinaigrette

salt and pepper

Place all the ingredients into a jar and shake to combine well. Season with salt and pepper to taste.

For other recipes that can be accompanied by cranberry relish see:

* Chicken Pot Pie – page 88
* BBQ Pork Pullapart – page 109
* Nutty Sausage Rolls – page 123

Chicken Taco Filo Cups

These awesome Chicken Taco Filo Cups are a twist on the traditional taco.
Kids will love eating them!

1 × 410 g can crushed tomatoes

½ packet taco seasoning (15 g)

12 filo pastry sheets, cut into 12 cm squares

1 egg, beaten

1 barbecued chicken, shredded

1 × 400 g can 4-bean mix

¾ cup guacamole

¾ cup sour cream

1½ cups grated tasty cheese

Preheat the oven to 180°C. Grease an 18-hole muffin tin. Mix the tomatoes and taco seasoning together in a bowl and set aside. Place two squares of filo pastry on top of each other and push into a hole in the muffin tin, allowing the pastry to overlap the edges of the hole. Now place another two sheets of pastry in the opposite direction in the hole. Brush with egg and repeat until all the holes are done. Cook in the oven for 5 minutes until just golden brown. Place a dessertspoonful each of the chicken, beans, tomato mixture, guacamole and sour cream into each of the pastry cups, then top with cheese. Return to oven for 5–10 minutes, until golden brown and the cheese has melted. Serve immediately.

* *

Freezing: Allow to cool to room temperature then wrap in aluminium foil, then in plastic wrap. Freeze for up to 2 months.

Thawing: Allow to sit in the fridge overnight or on the kitchen counter for up to an hour.

Reheating: Place in a preheated oven at 180°C for 10 minutes, or until hot.

Chicken and Vegetable Sausage Rolls

Here's a twist on the normal sausage rolls that everyone knows. Yummy finger food – nice and easy for entertaining! These are also perfect for lunch boxes – cut some small ones for the kids and some larger 'man-size' ones for hubby to take to work.

500 g chicken mince

1 cup wholemeal breadcrumbs

1 zucchini, grated

1 carrot, grated

½ brown onion, grated

2 tablespoons chopped fresh flat-leaf parsley (optional)

2 tablespoons finely chopped fresh spinach (optional)

1 teaspoon curry powder

2 eggs

2 sheets puff pastry

Preheat the oven to 180°C. In a large bowl, mix together all the ingredients except for one egg and the pastry until well combined. Divide the mixture in two and place a line of filling down the middle of each puff pastry sheet. Roll up then slice the sausage rolls on an angle (you can make them any size you wish). Beat the remaining egg and use a pastry brush to moisten the tops of the sausage rolls with the egg. Bake for 25 minutes or until golden brown.

* *

Freezing: Allow the cooked sausage rolls to cool to room temperature. Wrap in aluminium foil, then wrap in plastic wrap. Freeze for up to 2 months.

Thawing: Allow to sit in the fridge overnight or on the kitchen counter for up to an hour.

Reheating: Place in a preheated oven at 180°C for 10 minutes, or until hot.

Beef, Lamb and Pork

Traditionally, apart from the
odd steak, my family only really
eats beef during the winter months. So
when we do, it always tastes like a treat. Look
for rump steak, chuck steak, gravy beef and even
beef strips; these are all excellent casserole cuts.
For me, the world would truly be a sad place without
bacon – as far as I'm concerned, it is the food of the
gods. But, of course, pork comes in a lot of different
forms, and it is a very versatile meat, as is lamb.
I tend to go for cheaper cuts, like shoulder
and neck. They need to be cooked slowly
to break them down, but they are
so flavourful when done.

Beef Stock

Both beef and bacon stocks are good bases for beef casseroles and hearty stews. They are also used as a base for minestrone soup and many Asian dishes.

beef bones
(or bacon bones)

vegetables (onions, celery, carrots – whatever you have on hand)

Place the beef bones in a hot oven for 15 minutes. Cooking the bones in the oven enhances the meaty flavour and gives you a well-rounded, tasty stock. Place the bones and a heap of vegetables into a large saucepan and cover with water. Boil for approximately 4 hours (or cook in a slow cooker on high for 8 hours), skimming the 'scum' off the top every so often and discarding. Allow the stock to cool a little then strain well. Let the stock cool to room temperature before placing in the fridge for up to 7 days. This allows any fat to rise to the top – it can then be scooped off and discarded.

Freezing: Pour the stock into ice cube containers. Allow to freeze solid then remove and place in a ziplock bag. Freeze for up to 6 months.

Thawing: Don't thaw, add frozen as required.

Reheating: Place in a microwave-proof container or saucepan and heat until hot.

Beef Stroganoff

Beef Stroganoff is a firm family favourite in my house and is on a weekly rotation. I've always served it with crispy chips and freshly steamed vegetables, but some people have it on rice or pasta, which is nice too.

1 teaspoon butter

1 brown onion, finely chopped

2 cloves garlic, crushed

500 g rump steak, cut into thin strips

250 g mushrooms

3 tablespoons Worcestershire sauce

½ cup sour cream

1 tablespoon tomato paste

salt and pepper

Heat a frying pan over medium heat and add the butter. When bubbling, add the onion and garlic and fry until fragrant and softened. Add the steak and mushrooms and fry for 2–3 minutes or until just cooked. Add the Worcestershire sauce and cook for 2 minutes, turn the heat off and stir through the sour cream and the tomato paste. Season with salt and pepper to taste.

* *

Freezing: Make the stroganoff but don't add the sour cream (cream doesn't freeze well; it tends to separate and curdle). Allow the mixture to cool and three-quarters fill a ziplock bag. Freeze for up to 6 months.

Thawing: Allow to sit in the fridge for up to 24 hours.

Reheating: Place in a saucepan to heat through, add the sour cream and stir until the sauce thickens slightly.

Hints & Tips

* You could substitute chicken strips for the steak.

Beef and Cola Casserole

When I first read about this combination and people were raving about it, I was fairly sceptical, but when I gave it a go I was nicely surprised. The cola really makes the beef tender and the tomato paste thickens the sauce and adds a richness to the dish.

2 cloves garlic, crushed

1 × 40 g packet French onion soup mix

750 g gravy beef, cut into bite-sized pieces

1 × 375 ml can cola

2 tablespoons tomato paste

Add the garlic and French onion soup mix to the bottom of a slow cooker. Place the beef on top of the soup mix. Stir it well to evenly 'coat' the meat in the garlic and soup mix. Pour in the cola. Cook on high for 6 hours. Stir well and add the tomato paste – this will thicken the liquid and turn it into a casserole. Cook for a further 2 hours on low or until the meat starts to fall apart.

* *

Freezing: Allow to cool then three-quarters fill a ziplock bag. Freeze for up to 8 months.

Thawing: Allow to sit in the fridge for up to 24 hours.

Reheating: Place in a saucepan to heat through.

Hints & Tips

* To bulk up the recipe even further, add an onion in the beginning, and some chopped vegetables for the last 30 minutes.

Beef and Red Wine Casserole

Beef and Red Wine Casserole takes a little while to prepare and cook, but if you make the effort, the outcome is simply divine!

2 tablespoons olive oil

1.5 kg gravy beef, cut into bite-sized pieces

6 cloves garlic, crushed

5 rashers bacon, diced

3 carrots, sliced

3 brown onions, diced

2 sticks celery, sliced

125 g button mushrooms, chopped

1 cup red wine

1 cup beef stock

2 tablespoons cornflour

Preheat the oven to 160°C. Heat the oil in a large heavy-based pan and brown the beef in batches until well browned all over. Remove the beef from the pot. Add the garlic, bacon, carrot, onion, celery and mushrooms to the pot. Cook on high for approximately 5 minutes, or until starting to brown. Stir in the red wine. Simmer uncovered until the mixture is reduced by half. Add the stock and 1 cup of water. Put the beef into a casserole dish and pour in the red wine mixture. Cook in the oven, covered, for approximately 2 hours or until the meat starts to fall apart when separated with a fork. If the casserole appears too wet, dissolve the cornflour in a little water and stir through until thickened.

SLOW COOKER VERSION
Brown the beef, then add all the ingredients except for the cornflour to the slow cooker. Cook on low for 6–8 hours. Thicken with the cornflour if required.

Freezing: Allow to cool then three-quarters fill a ziplock bag. Freeze for up to 8 months.

Thawing: Allow to sit in the fridge for up to 24 hours.

Reheating: Place in a saucepan to heat through.

Country Beef Casserole with Herb Scones

You can also make this dish in the slow cooker. Cook the beef mixture on low for 7–8 hours. Don't add the scones; bake them on a lined baking tray at 180°C for 12 minutes.

1 kg gravy beef, cut into bite-sized pieces

¼ cup plain flour

3 tablespoons oil

4 medium brown onions, roughly chopped

2 cloves garlic, crushed

⅓ cup plum jam

⅓ cup brown vinegar

1 cup beef stock

2 teaspoons sweet chilli sauce

HERB SCONES

2 cups self-raising flour

30 g butter

2 tablespoons chopped chives

2 tablespoons chopped parsley

¾ cup milk

Preheat the oven to 180°C. Toss the beef in the flour until well coated. Heat the oil in a heavy-based saucepan and brown the meat in batches. Remove and place in a casserole dish. Reheat the oil and add the onion and garlic, and cook until soft. Place on top of the beef. In a bowl, combine the plum jam, vinegar, stock and chilli sauce. Pour over the beef. Cover in foil and bake for 1½ hours, or until the beef is very tender. Meanwhile, to make the herb scones, sift the flour into a bowl, then rub in the butter with your fingertips until the mixture resembles breadcrumbs. Add the herbs and milk, and stir until just combined. Turn onto a floured surface and knead lightly until smooth. Use scone cutters to cut out the scones. Uncover the casserole dish and place the herb scones on top of the meat. Bake for a further 30 minutes, or until the scones are golden brown.

Freezing: Place in an aluminium foil container (or freezer-to-oven container) and cover in plastic wrap. Freeze for up to 6 months.

Thawing: Allow to sit in the fridge for up to 24 hours.

Reheating: Place a lid on the container and reheat in the oven at 180°C for 20 minutes or until heated through.

Cheesy Beef Puffs

Cheesy Beef Puffs are brilliant for using up leftover mince, when making Savoury Mince, for example (page 69), or the Bulk Bolognaise Sauce (page 68).

1 cup leftover beef mince (cooked)

½ cup cream cheese

½ cup grated tasty cheese

2 sheets puff pastry

Preheat the oven to 200°C. In a large bowl, combine the mince and cheeses. Cut each piece of pastry into 16 pieces (cut into quarters then cut each quarter into quarters). Place a teaspoonful of mince mixture into the centre of each piece then fold over to form a triangle. Press the edges firmly together. Place on a baking tray and bake for 15–20 minutes, or until golden.

* *

Freezing: Cheesy Beef Puffs can be frozen cooked or uncooked. To freeze uncooked, place on baking paper and double wrap in plastic wrap. Freeze for up to 2 months. To freeze cooked, allow to cool then wrap in aluminium foil and plastic wrap. Freeze for up to 6 months.

Thawing: Allow both raw and cooked puffs to defrost in the fridge overnight or on the kitchen counter for up to an hour.

Reheating: For raw Cheesy Beef Puffs, cook as above. For the cooked version, place in a preheated oven at 180°C for 8–10 minutes.

Hints & Tips

* You can serve the puffs with chutney or relish.

Steak Normanby

Steak Normanby is a recipe that has been handed down through the generations in my family. It is perfect for a big family dinner or for a gathering of friends. It only uses basic ingredients that everyone will either have in their cupboard or be able to get their hands on without any fuss. It is so delicious you'll be mopping up the sauce with pieces of fresh bread.

2 tablespoons plain flour

2 teaspoons sugar

2 kg gravy beef, cut into bite-sized pieces

3 large brown onions, sliced into rings

2 cloves garlic, crushed

1 tablespoon Worcestershire sauce

2 tablespoons tomato sauce

2 tablespoons white vinegar

½ cup beef stock

3 bacon rashers, thinly sliced

Preheat the oven to 180°C. Place the flour, sugar and beef in a plastic bag and shake to coat the meat well. Line the bottom of a deep casserole dish with three-quarters of the onion rings and sprinkle the garlic over the top. Place the floured meat on top of that. In a jug, mix together the sauces, vinegar and stock and pour carefully over the meat. Then top with the bacon and remaining onion slices. Cover and cook for 2–2½ hours. Take the lid off for the last 10 minutes to crisp the bacon.

* *

Freezing: Allow to cool then three-quarters fill a ziplock bag. Freeze for up to 8 months.

Thawing: Allow to sit in the fridge for up to 24 hours.

Reheating: Place in a saucepan to heat through.

Irish Stew

Irish Stew is a yummy filling meal for a family, and it won't break the bank.

¼ cup plain flour

1.2 kg lamb neck chops, trimmed

¼ cup olive oil

1 brown onion, finely chopped

1 tablespoon fresh thyme leaves

2 carrots, peeled and sliced

1 kg desirée potatoes, peeled and cut into 2 cm pieces

6 cups beef stock

crusty bread, to serve

Place the flour and chops in a plastic bag. Shake and make sure the lamb is coated well. Put 1 tablespoon of the oil in a frying pan and cook the onion and thyme until the onion is golden. Set aside. Cook the lamb in the same pan with the remaining oil in two batches, making sure the meat is browned on all sides (this ensures that the lamb is sealed). In a large saucepan layer the lamb, onion mixture, carrots and potatoes. Pour in the stock and bring to the boil. Reduce the heat, cover and simmer for 1½ hours. Skim any fat off the top as it appears. Take the lid off and let it simmer for another 30 minutes, until the lamb is nice and tender and the sauce has thickened slightly. Serve with crusty bread for mopping up the sauce.

Freezing: Allow the stew to cool then three-quarters fill a ziplock bag. Freeze for up to 8 months.

Thawing: Allow to sit in the fridge for up to 24 hours.

Reheating: Place in a saucepan to heat through.

Hints & Tips

* You can use diced beef instead of lamb.

Lamb Muffin Pies

These pies are delicious and quick and easy to put on the table, particularly if you are using leftover roast lamb.

2 rashers bacon, diced

¼ cup gravy mix

1½ cups water

1 tablespoon Worcestershire sauce

2 cups cooked lamb, diced (we used leftover roast lamb)

6 sheets puff pastry

¾ cup grated cheese

1 egg, beaten

Preheat the oven to 180°C. Grease muffin tins (enough so you have 18 holes). Fry the bacon until just browned. Remove from the heat. Place the gravy mix in a saucepan and slowly add the water, whisking until smooth. Place over medium heat and continue to whisk until the gravy thickens. Stir in the Worcestershire sauce. Add the lamb and bacon and stir through. Use a cookie cutter or a large glass to cut 18 circles out of pastry, big enough to line the holes in your muffin tins. Press into the holes, then add 1 heaped tablespoon of the meat and gravy and top with 2 teaspoons of grated cheese. Cut out circles from the pastry the diameter of the holes. Place a pastry 'lid' on each pie and brush with egg. Bake for 25 minutes.

Freezing: Allow to cool and place on baking paper in an airtight container. Loosely cover with baking paper before sealing. Freeze for up to 3 months.

Thawing: Allow the pies to stand on the kitchen counter for an hour before cooking.

Reheating: Place in a preheated oven at 180°C for 15–20 minutes, or until hot.

BBQ Pork Pullapart

This is a great recipe for having on hand to fill a fresh bread roll. It also works as a meal served with mashed potato and seasonal vegies.

1 onion, sliced into rings

2 tablespoons plain flour

1 pork shoulder

2 cloves garlic, crushed

¾ cup barbecue sauce

1 teaspoon chilli powder

1 teaspoon cumin

Place the onion into the bottom of a slow cooker and sprinkle the flour over the top. Add the pork shoulder. In a cup, combine the garlic, barbecue sauce, chilli powder and cumin. Slather the sauce over the roast. Cover and cook on low for 8 hours. Remove the pork and shred. Serve with some of the cooking sauce spooned over the top.

Freezing: Allow to cool and three-quarters fill a ziplock bag. Freeze for up to 6 months.

Thawing: Allow to sit on the kitchen counter for 10–15 minutes.

Reheating: Pan fry until heated through.

Mushroom and Bacon Mini Quiches

These quiches are great for breakfast or lunch. This recipe is versatile so you can experiment with many flavour combinations. Use up leftover roast vegies or meat or fill with salmon and fetta. Maybe try the old favourite, ham and tomato.

3 sheets frozen puff pastry, thawed

75 g butter

400 g button mushrooms, sliced

2 cloves garlic, crushed

2 rashers bacon, diced

4 eggs

½ cup cream or milk

salt and pepper

½ cup grated tasty cheese

Preheat the oven to 210°C. Lightly grease a 12-hole muffin tin. Use a jar or cutter to cut out four circles from each pastry sheet, large enough to line the muffin holes. (Alternatively, just cut the pastry square into equal quarters, which will give the quiches a more rustic appearance.) Line each hole with pastry and make a small cross in the bottom of each with a bread knife, for even cooking. Melt the butter in a frying pan and fry the mushrooms and garlic until golden brown. Remove from the pan and set aside. Cook the bacon in the same pan until just crisp and combine with the mushrooms. Divide the mixture between the muffin holes. Whisk the eggs and cream or milk together in a jug and season with salt and pepper to taste. Pour the egg mixture evenly between all 12 holes and top with the cheese. Bake for 25 minutes, or until the pastry is golden and the cheese melted.

Freezing: Allow to cool then place in a ziplock bag and store on a flat surface. Freeze for up to 2 weeks.

Thawing: Allow to sit in the fridge overnight or on the kitchen counter for 30 minutes.

Reheating: Microwave for 10 seconds or place in a preheated oven at 180°C for 8 minutes, or until heated through.

Bacon and Egg Pie

This recipe is my beautiful mum's. I've eaten it all my life and now I make it for my family. It's also great cold for lunches the next day. Add as many or as few vegies as you like.

canola oil spray

2 sheets puff pastry

500 g bacon, diced

1 brown onion, finely diced

vegies such as sliced mushrooms, chopped capsicum, grated zucchini, grated carrot, canned peas, corn etc.

6 eggs

1 × 375 ml can evaporated milk (normal milk is fine if you don't have any evaporated)

salt and pepper

1 cup grated tasty cheese

Preheat the oven to 180°C. Spray a deep baking tray with canola oil. Line the baking tray with the pastry (overlapping slightly), making sure it has no holes and goes at least 2 centimetres up the sides of the tray. Fry the bacon and onion until almost crispy (if you are adding any other vegies, throw them in too so they are cooked through). Spread evenly over the pastry. Whisk together the eggs and evaporated milk, then season with salt and pepper to taste. Pour the mixture carefully into the baking tray. Sprinkle the cheese over the top and bake for 30 minutes or until set and golden on top.

* *

Freezing: Wrap slices in plastic wrap and store on a flat surface. Freeze for up to 2 weeks.

Thawing: Allow to sit in the fridge overnight or on the kitchen counter for 30 minutes.

Reheating: Microwave for 1 minute or place in a preheated oven at 180°C for 8 minutes, or until heated through.

Vegetarian

I love vegetarian food, but
it seems to take a long time to
prepare to get the taste just right. With
freezer cooking, you can take the time to
cook terrific and healthy vegetarian meals so
they only need to be reheated! If your family
isn't really into vegetarian food, please try the
I Can't Believe It's Not Mince Lasagne – I fooled
my whole family and serve it regularly.
If you puree some vegies to add to the
sauce you can get even more nutrients
into your family meals!

Chickpea Curry

This spicy dish works well as a side or a main and is an ideal winter warmer. Chickpeas are a helpful source of zinc, folate and protein, and are low in fat. They have also been found to assist with lowering cholesterol. Cutting down on your meat consumption by serving up a few vegetarian dishes like this one during the week can add up to plenty of savings when shopping.

1½ tablespoons olive oil

1 medium onion, chopped

1 medium green capsicum, chopped

2 cloves garlic, crushed

1½ tablespoons curry powder

1 tablespoon malt vinegar

1 × 400 g can chopped tomatoes

600 g canned chickpeas, drained and rinsed

3 medium potatoes, diced

⅓ cup natural yoghurt

Heat the oil in a large saucepan over medium heat. Cook the onion, capsicum, garlic and curry powder, stirring, until the onion is soft. Add the vinegar, tomatoes (undrained), chickpeas and potato. Simmer, covered, for about 20 minutes, or until the potato is tender, stirring occasionally. Serve with a dollop of yoghurt.

Freezing: Allow to cool to room temperature then three-quarters fill a ziplock bag and store on a flat surface. Freeze for up to 2 months.

Thawing: Allow to sit in the fridge for up to 24 hours.

Reheating: Place in a saucepan to heat through or reheat in the microwave, stirring every minute, until hot.

I Can't Believe It's Not Mince Lasagne

My husband loves his meat and thinks vegetarian food is for tree-hugging hippies. But when I served him what I call 'I Can't Believe It's Not Mince Lasagne', he didn't even know it was meat-free! I like to serve it with fresh salad and Garlic Bread (page 142).

1 × 435 g can refried beans

1 × 410 g can crushed tomatoes

½ cup red lentils

1 tablespoon Italian herbs

canola oil, for greasing

½ packet lasagne sheets (125 g)

Cheese Sauce (see page 71)

1 cup grated tasty cheese

Preheat the oven to 180°C. Combine the refried beans, tomatoes, lentils and Italian herbs in a bowl. Grease the bottom of a deep baking dish with canola oil. Spoon in enough of the refried bean mix to just cover the bottom of the baking dish. Add lasagne sheets to cover the beans without the sheets overlapping. Add a layer of cheese sauce on top. Keep stacking the layers in that order until you run out of ingredients. Top with the grated cheese and bake for 40 minutes, or until cooked through and golden on top.

* *

Freezing: Allow to cool and cut into slices. Place into an aluminium tray and seal with the cardboard lid. Freeze for up to 2 months.

Thawing: Allow to sit in the fridge overnight.

Reheating: Place the aluminium tray in a pre-heated oven at 180°C for 25 minutes. Remove the cardboard lid for the last 5 minutes to brown.

Lentil and Pumpkin Lasagne

So many vegetables in one dish! Low fat and easy to do, Lentil and Pumpkin Lasagne is sure to become a favourite in your house.

olive oil spray

1 large brown onion, finely chopped

2 cloves garlic, crushed

¼ cup white wine

400 g pumpkin, cooked and pureed

1 × 400 g can lentils, drained and rinsed

2 × 400 g cans chopped tomatoes

2 tablespoons olives, finely chopped

1 cup salt-reduced vegetable stock

½ bunch flat-leaf parsley, chopped

salt and pepper

3 sheets fresh lasagne (100 g total)

60 g reduced-fat fetta cheese, crumbled

rocket leaves, to serve

Preheat the oven to 180°C. Grease a baking dish with olive oil. In a saucepan over medium heat, sauté the onion for 5 minutes or until coloured. Add the garlic, wine, pumpkin, lentils, tomatoes, olives and stock. Bring to the boil. Reduce the heat and simmer for 25 minutes. Remove from the heat, and add the parsley. Season with salt and pepper to taste. Spread a quarter of the lentil mixture over the base of the baking dish, then top with a lasagne sheet. Repeat twice, and spread the remaining lentil mix over the top of the last lasagne sheet. Sprinkle the fetta over the top. Bake for 25–30 minutes, or until cooked through. Allow to stand for 5 minutes before serving. Serve with rocket leaves alongside.

* *

Freezing: Allow to cool then cut into slices. Place in an aluminium foil container (or freezer-to-oven container) and cover with the cardboard lid. Freeze for up to 2 months.

Thawing: Allow to sit in the fridge overnight.

Reheating: Place the aluminium tray in a preheated oven at 180°C for 25 minutes. Remove the cardboard lid for the last 5 minutes to brown.

Thai Pumpkin Couscous Fritters

These are a lovely alternative to the Corn Fritters we often make (page 129).
Served with a dollop of yoghurt, they are divine!

1 cup cubed pumpkin

½ cup olive oil

salt and pepper

1¼ cups water

1 cup uncooked couscous

3 shallots, thinly sliced

2 tablespoons plain flour

1 tablespoon Thai seasoning

2 eggs, beaten

green salad, to serve

Greek yoghurt, to serve

Preheat the oven to 200°C. Place the pumpkin cubes onto a baking tray and drizzle with a tablespoon of the olive oil. Season with salt and pepper to taste. Roast for 15–20 minutes, or until brown. Bring the water to the boil in a saucepan, add the couscous and remove from the heat. Cover with a lid and let stand for 5 minutes. Fluff up the couscous with a fork then allow to cool slightly. Place the shallots into a mixing bowl, add the flour and Thai seasoning and mix well. Add the eggs and mix to combine, then add the couscous and pumpkin and gently toss through. Roll into eight fritters. Heat the remaining oil over medium–high heat then cook the fritters for 2–3 minutes each side, turning when golden brown. Drain on paper towel. Serve with a green salad and Greek yoghurt as a dipping sauce.

Freezing: Allow to cool to room temperature then layer on baking paper in an airtight container. Freeze for up to 2 weeks.

Thawing: Do not thaw; cook from frozen.

Reheating: Pan fry until heated through.

Hints & Tips

∗ Keep refrigerated for 4 days once cooked.

Easy Potato Gnocchi

This recipe is surprisingly easy and, of course, it tastes just divine. Serve with a burnt butter sauce or a simple bolognaise (page 68)

1 kg desirée potatoes, peeled, cooked and mashed well

1 egg

300 g plain flour

salt and pepper

nutmeg (optional)

Place the mashed potato in a bowl and add the rest of the ingredients. Knead lightly to form a firm dough. Divide the dough into six portions and roll each out like a sausage on a floured surface. Cut each 'sausage' into 2 cm pieces to create the gnocchi. Heat a large pot of salted water until boiling. Drop the gnocchi into the boiling water (in batches so you don't crowd the pot) and cook for 3–4 minutes, until the gnocchi float to the top. Remove and drain well.

Freezing: Place uncooked gnocchi into a ziplock bag. Freeze for up to 2 months.

Thawing: Do not thaw; cook from frozen.

Reheating: Cook as above.

Bean and Vegie Quesadillas

Quesadillas can be a little bit fiddly to make, but you do end up with a very nice lunch or dinner. They are a great way to get extra vegies into your hubby's and kids' diet!

1 tablespoon olive oil

1 brown onion, finely diced

2 cloves garlic, crushed

1 large carrot, grated

½ capsicum (any colour), deseeded and finely chopped

2 tomatoes, chopped

1 x 400 g can red kidney beans, drained, rinsed and roughly mashed

½ teaspoon sugar

½ teaspoon ground cumin

1 tablespoon barbecue sauce

10 flour tortillas

grated tasty cheese

1 avocado, sliced (optional)

Heat the oil in a large frying pan over medium–high heat. Add the onion and cook for a couple of minutes, stirring often. Pop in the garlic, carrot and capsicum and continue cooking for 3 minutes. Add the tomato, beans, sugar, cumin and barbecue sauce. Cook for another couple of minutes. Warm the tortillas in the oven or microwave according to the packet directions. Spread a fifth of the bean mixture over one tortilla. Top with cheese and avocado slices, if using. Place another tortilla on top and slide into a warm non-stick frying pan over medium heat. Cook until golden on the bottom (4–5 minutes), then slide out onto a plate and flip over. Return to the pan and cook until both sides are golden. Repeat with the remaining tortillas.

Freezing: Allow to cool to room temperature, wrap in baking paper then in plastic wrap. Freeze for up to 2 weeks.

Thawing: Pop into lunch boxes frozen. Alternatively, allow to sit on the kitchen counter (unwrapped) for 20 minutes.

Reheating: Microwave for 15 seconds, or until hot.

Pasta and Pesto

Homemade pesto is a great stand-by to have in the freezer. There are so many different types of homemade pesto sauce you can make – this is my favourite.

1 × 500 g packet pasta

2 cups fresh basil leaves

¼ cup lightly toasted cashews (or walnuts)

2 cloves garlic, coarsely chopped

pinch of salt

⅓ cup cold-pressed olive oil

½ cup grated parmesan cheese, plus extra for sprinkling

Boil a large saucepan of water. Cook the pasta according to the packet instructions. In a food processor, combine the basil, cashews, garlic and salt. With the processor running, slowly pour in the olive oil and then add the cheese. Stir the pesto through the cooked pasta and sprinkle with parmesan.

* *

Freezing: Spoon pesto into greased ice cube containers and cover with plastic wrap. Freeze for up to 12 months.

Thawing: Do not thaw; cook from frozen.

Sour Cream Quiche

This recipe only contains three ingredients! It works well as is, but you can also add a whole range of extra ingredients if you wish. I love it with broccoli, but of course you can add bacon, onion, grated cheese, mushrooms, corn, capsicum – whatever you like.

1 sheet puff pastry

3 eggs

300 ml sour cream

salt and pepper (optional)

Preheat the oven to 180°C. Grease a pie dish then line with the puff pastry. Whisk together the eggs and sour cream and season with salt and pepper to taste, if using. Add any extra ingredients, if you wish, and pour into the pastry shell. Bake for 30–35 minutes, or until golden and set.

* *

Freezing: Allow to cool then cut into serving portions. Double wrap in plastic wrap and store on a flat surface. Freeze for up to 2 weeks.

Thawing: Allow to sit in the fridge overnight or on the kitchen counter for 30 minutes.

Reheating: Microwave for 10 seconds or place in a preheated oven at 180°C for 8 minutes, or until heated through.

Hints & Tips

* I like to serve this quiche with a garden salad and crusty bread, but boiled potatoes are a good accompaniment as well.

Soybean Burgers

When you want a burger, but want to be vegetarian, this recipe gives you the answer. It's simply packed with flavour.

1 × 410 g can soybeans, drained and rinsed

1 brown onion, chopped

2 sticks celery, chopped

1 tablespoon tahini

1 carrot, grated

3 tablespoons olive oil

Coarsely blend the soybeans, onion, celery and tahini together. Mix in the grated carrot and form into patties. Place the oil in a frying pan over medium heat and fry the patties until golden and cooked through, turning once (about 4 minutes each side).

Freezing: Layer uncooked burgers on sheets of baking paper in an airtight container. Freeze for up to 2 months.

Thawing: Do not thaw; cook from frozen.

Reheating: Pan fry until crispy on the outside and well cooked in the middle.

Nutty Sausage Rolls

These are great to have on hand in the freezer for when guests turn up. They also make a complete meal alongside mashed potato and salad. I like to serve them with a chutney or sweet chilli sauce for dipping. Delissimo!

3 eggs

½ cup shelled pecans or walnuts

1 brown onion, roughly chopped

1 tablespoon tamari (Japanese soy sauce)

250 g ricotta, cottage or fetta cheese

150 g fresh chopped zucchini, broccoli, red capsicum, carrot (any vegies you like)

½ cup breadcrumbs

1 cup rolled oats

2 tablespoons dried mixed herbs

1 teaspoon sea salt

2 butter puff pastry sheets

milk, for brushing

sesame seeds, for decorating (optional)

Preheat the oven to 180°C. Place the eggs, nuts, onion, tamari, cheese and vegies into a blender and blend until well combined. Mix the breadcrumbs, oats, herbs and salt together in a large bowl. Add the vegetable mixture and combine well. Allow to sit for 10 minutes. Cut the pastry sheets in half. You need to work quickly with butter pastry as once it thaws to room temperature it can be hard to work with. Keep as cold as possible to make rolling easier. Divide the vegetable mixture between the pastry rectangles, placing it along one long edge of each piece. Roll the pastry up around the mixture, like you were rolling sushi. Brush with milk and sprinkle with sesame seeds, if using. Cut to your preferred size and place on a baking tray. Bake for 15–20 minutes, or until golden and cooked through.

* *

Freezing: Allow to cool to room temperature then layer on baking paper in an airtight container. Freeze for up to 2 months.

Thawing: Do not thaw; cook from frozen.

Reheating: Place in a preheated oven at 150°C for 15 minutes, or until heated through.

Snacks

If your kids are always complaining that there is 'never anything in the house to eat' – then this section is for you. Snacks don't necessarily mean unhealthy, and we have a great choice of both sweet and savoury 'instant meals' that will fill tummies big and small. Best of all, most of them can be popped straight from the freezer into lunch boxes, making mornings even easier!

Bulk Savoury Muffins

Want to make enough savoury muffins to last two school kids a whole month for less than 17 cents per muffin? Try our Bulk Savoury Muffins. They are made with fresh vegetables, are healthy and freezable, and will make a great addition to lunch boxes. Perfect for breakfast on the run too! This recipe makes 60 muffins.

3 cups self-raising flour

2 cups wholemeal self-raising flour

1 teaspoon salt

3 eggs

3½ cups milk

2 zucchini, grated (skin on)

2 large potatoes, peeled and grated

2 brown onions, grated

3 carrots, grated

1½ cups ham or bacon pieces (optional)

1 cup grated cheddar cheese

Preheat the oven to 200°C. Line muffin tins with paper cases (as this recipe does have a tendency to 'stick' – the cases also make the muffins more portable). Sift the flours and salt together into a bowl and make a well in the centre. In a separate bowl combine the egg and milk. Pour the liquid slowly into the well in the flour mixture, using a whisk to bring the batter together. Be careful not to overwork the batter. Add the grated vegetables and ham, if using, and mix with a wooden spoon until just combined. The mixture should be sticky. Spoon into the muffin cases so they are three-quarters full and top with a pinch of cheese. Bake for 20–25 minutes, or until golden and cooked through.

Freezing: Allow to cool then place in a ziplock bag. Freeze for up to 2 months.

Thawing: Pop into lunch boxes frozen. Alternatively, allow to sit on the kitchen counter for 5 minutes.

Reheating: If you want your muffins hot, heat in the microwave for 8 seconds each.

Spinach and Fetta Muffins

These Spinach and Fetta Muffins would make a great snack for St Patrick's Day. Green, cheesy deliciousness!

150 g plain flour

100 g plain wholemeal flour

3 teaspoons baking powder

1 teaspoon salt

200 g frozen spinach, thawed and chopped

2 eggs, beaten

80 ml olive oil

300 ml milk

180 g fetta cheese (fat-reduced is fine), cubed

Preheat the oven to 180°C. Line a 12-hole muffin tin with paper cases. Sift the flours together into a bowl and add the baking powder and salt. In another bowl, combine the spinach, eggs, olive oil and milk. Add in the flour mixture and stir, but do not over-mix. Fold in the fetta. Divide the mixture between the holes in the muffin tin and bake for 20 minutes, or until golden.

* *

Freezing: Allow to cool to room temperature then layer on baking paper in an airtight container. Freeze for up to 2 months.

Thawing: Pop into lunch boxes frozen. Alternatively, allow to sit on the kitchen counter for 5 minutes.

Reheating: If you want the muffins warm, microwave for 8–10 seconds on high, or until warm.

Ham and Vegetable Muffins

Looking for a fantastic savoury snack? These Ham and Vegetable Muffins are packed full of vegies and taste great!

½ cup milk

3 eggs

60 g butter, melted then cooled

2 cups self-raising flour

1 large carrot, peeled and grated

1 zucchini, grated

100 g ham, chopped

1¼ cups grated cheese

Preheat the oven to 160°C. Grease a 12-hole muffin tin. Add the wet ingredients to the dry in a large bowl. Divide the mixture between the holes in the muffin tin. Bake for 30 minutes, or until a skewer inserted into the centre comes out clean (bearing in mind that the cheese will be melted and may end up on the skewer).

* *

Freezing: Allow to cool to room temperature then layer on baking paper in an airtight container. Freeze for up to 2 months.

Thawing: Pop into lunch boxes frozen. Alternatively, allow to sit on the kitchen counter for 5 minutes.

Reheating: If you want the muffins warm, microwave for 8–10 seconds on high, or until warm.

Hints & Tips

* You can also make these muffins with peas and corn instead of carrot and zucchini.

Corn Fritters

Corn Fritters are great for breakfast, lunch, a light dinner or a snack.
This is a good recipe to whip up when you don't feel much like cooking!

2 fresh corncobs

100 g self-raising flour

pinch of salt

1 tablespoon butter, melted

1 egg

3 tablespoons milk

canola oil

tomato salsa, to serve

Using a sharp knife, cut the corn kernels off the cobs (alternatively, you can use a drained medium can of super sweet corn kernels). In a bowl, combine the flour, salt, butter and egg. Add the milk and the corn kernels and mix to form a thick batter. Heat a heavy-based frying pan and add a little canola oil. Drop in dessertspoonfuls of batter and cook until golden on both sides. Drain on paper towel and serve hot with some tomato salsa.

* *

Freezing: Allow to cool to room temperature then layer on baking paper in an airtight container. Freeze for up to 1 month.

Thawing: Do not thaw; cook from frozen.

Reheating: Pan fry until heated through or place in a preheated oven at 200°C for 5 minutes. (Don't microwave, as they will go soggy.)

Hints & Tips

* For a spicy version, add a teaspoon of chopped red chilli.

Cheesy Vegemite Scrolls

Mmmm … cheese and Vegemite. A classic combination.

3 cups self-raising flour

pinch of salt

50 g butter

375 ml milk

1–2 tablespoons Vegemite

200 g cheddar cheese, grated

Preheat the oven to 220°C. Line a bakng tray with baking paper. Sift the flour and salt together into a bowl. Rub in the butter with your fingertips until the mixture resembles breadcrumbs. Stir in enough milk to make a soft dough. Knead on a lightly floured board. Roll out to form a rectangle roughly 40 by 25 centimetres. Spread Vegemite over the dough using a blunt knife. Sprinkle three-quarters of the cheese over the top. Roll up the dough starting from a long edge. Cut 10 4-centimetre pieces from the roll. Place on the baking tray. Sprinkle the rest of the cheese over the top. Bake in the oven for 15–20 minutes, or until golden.

* *

Freezing: Allow to cool to room temperature then wrap in plastic wrap and store on a flat surface. Freeze for up to 2 months.

Thawing: Pop into lunch boxes frozen. Alternatively, allow to sit on the kitchen counter for 5 minutes.

Reheating: If you want the scrolls warm, microwave for 12–15 seconds on high, or until warm.

Hints & Tips

  * If making and eating fresh, keep for no longer than 2 days.

Pizza Scrolls

I love Pizza Scrolls – they are perfect for school lunches or a snack on the go.

3 cups self-raising flour

pinch of salt

50 g butter

1 cup milk

½ cup diced ham
(or bacon)

¼ cup pineapple
chunks

200 g cheddar cheese,
grated

Preheat the oven to 220°C. Grease a baking tray. Sift the flour and salt together into a bowl. Rub in the butter with your fingertips until the mixture resembles breadcrumbs. Stir in enough milk to make a soft dough. Knead on a lightly floured board until the dough is smooth. Roll out to form a rectangle roughly 40 by 25 centimetres. Spread the ham and pineapple over the dough. Sprinkle three-quarters of the cheese over the top. Roll up the dough from a long edge. Cut the roll into 4 centimetre pieces (you should get about 10). Place, cut side up, on the baking tray. Sprinkle the rest of the cheese over the top. Bake for 15–20 minutes, or until golden.

* *

Freezing: Allow to cool to room temperature then layer on baking paper in an airtight container. Freeze for up to 2 months.

Thawing: Pop into lunch boxes frozen. Alternatively, allow to sit on the kitchen counter for 5 minutes.

Reheating: If you want the scrolls warm, microwave for 12–15 seconds on high, or until warm.

Hints & Tips

* To make a puff pastry version, substitute a sheet of pre-made puff pastry for the dough – extra quick! Just watch them to make sure they don't overcook!

Mince Scrolls

If you are a fan of our other scroll recipes, you'll love this hearty, beefy mince version!

1 tablespoon olive oil

1 brown onion, finely chopped

1 clove garlic, crushed

300 g beef, chicken, pork or turkey mince

1 × 400 g can diced tomatoes

1 tablespoon tomato paste

2 tablespoons Worcestershire sauce

½ cup beef stock

2 cups self-raising flour

1 teaspoon white sugar

3 tablespoons butter

¾ cup milk

1 cup grated cheddar cheese

Preheat the oven to 180°C. Line a baking tray with baking paper. Heat the olive oil in a frying pan and cook the onion and garlic until the onion is soft. Add the mince and cook until browned. Add the tomatoes, tomato paste, Worcestershire sauce and stock and simmer for 25 minutes, or until the mixture reduces and thickens. Remove from the heat and cool to room temperature. Combine the flour and sugar in a bowl and rub in the butter with your fingertips until the mixture resembles breadcrumbs. Stir in the milk and mix to a sticky dough-like consistency. Knead on a floured surface and roll out to a 40 by 30 centimetres rectangle. Spread the mince mixture over the dough and sprinkle with the cheese. Roll up the dough from a long edge and cut into 12 scrolls. Place the scrolls on the baking tray, giving them a little room to spread. Bake for 25 minutes, or until golden.

* *

Freezing: Allow to cool to room temperature then layer on baking paper in an airtight container. Freeze for up to 2 months.

Thawing: Pop into lunch boxes frozen. Alternatively, allow to sit on the kitchen counter for 5 minutes.

Reheating: If you want the scrolls warm, microwave for 12–15 seconds on high, or until warm.

Cinnamon Scrolls

Cinnamon Scrolls are easy to prepare and are best eaten warm from the oven and dripping in icing. Mmm ... I can feel my thighs getting closer together.

2 cups self-raising flour

pinch of salt

185 g butter

⅔ cup milk

4 tablespoons brown sugar

3 teaspoons cinnamon

1 cup icing sugar

2–3 tablespoons water

Preheat the oven to 200°C. Line a baking tray with baking paper. Sift the flour and salt together into a bowl. Rub 85 grams of the butter into the flour with your fingertips until the mixture resembles breadcrumbs, then add the milk and cut the mixture together with a knife, so the ingredients are well combined. Place the dough onto a lightly floured surface and knead until the dough is smooth. Roll into a rectangle roughly 30 by 30 centimetres and about half a centimetre thick. Combine the butter, brown sugar and cinnamon and mix to make a spread. Paste over the entire surface of the dough, roll up the dough from a long edge and cut into 2.5 cm pieces. Place the scrolls onto the lined baking tray, allowing enough room for them to double in size. Bake for 12–14 minutes, or until golden brown. Combine the icing sugar and water in a bowl to make a glaze and drizzle over the hot scrolls.

Freezing: Allow to cool to room temperature then layer on baking paper in an airtight container. Freeze for up to 2 months.

Thawing: Pop into lunch boxes frozen. Alternatively, allow to sit on the kitchen counter for 5 minutes.

Reheating: If you want the scrolls warm, microwave for 12–15 seconds on high, or until warm.

Frozen Banana Yoghurt Pops

A tasty and nutritious snack the kids will enjoy anytime. Easy to make and fun to eat – they are also a good option for birthday parties!

1 banana, cut into five equal pieces

1 small tub fruit yoghurt

hundreds and thousands

Grab five paddle pop sticks and insert deeply into the pieces of banana. Dip the banana pieces halfway into the fruit yoghurt, then roll in the hundreds and thousands. Place upright on a sheet of baking paper and freeze for 10 minutes.

Freezing: Place into a ziplock bag. Freeze for up to 2 months.

Thawing: Not suitable for thawing. Eat frozen.

Hints & Tips

* Alternative flavours to dip your banana pop into include muesli, crushed nuts or Milo.

Raw Apricot Slice

This egg-free, dairy-free, gluten-free slice with no added sugar is a healthy substitute for muesli bars in lunch boxes. Good for when you're eating clean!

250 g dried apricots

1 cup desiccated coconut, plus extra for sprinkling

1 cup almond meal

3 tablespoons coconut oil

Line a slice tray with baking paper. Place the apricots in a jug and cover with water. Let them soak for an hour and then drain. Place all the ingredients into a food processor and pulse until the mixture is the consistency of breadcrumbs. Press the mixture into the slice tray and sprinkle with a little additional coconut. Chill for at least 3 hours or overnight. Cut into slices to serve.

Freezing: Wrap in plastic wrap and store on a flat surface. Freeze for up to 1 month.

Thawing: Pop into lunch boxes frozen. Alternatively, allow to sit on the kitchen counter for 5 minutes.

Hints & Tips

* Coconut oil is readily available at most supermarkets or health food stores.
* To make this recipe nut-free, substitute the wheatgerm for the almond meal.

Saucy Cheese Slice

If you're a fan of savoury slices and of cheesy goodness, then this is a new one for you to try. It makes a nice snack, or can be served as a light lunch or dinner with a salad. Delish!

BASE

canola oil spray

1 cup self-raising flour

1½ tablespoons butter, at room temperature

pinch of salt

¾ cup grated tasty cheese

CHEESE SAUCE TOPPING

1 egg, separated

1½ tablespoons butter

1 small onion, grated

1 tablespoon plain flour

1 cup milk

1 cup grated tasty cheese

pinch of salt

Preheat the oven to 180°C. Line a slice tin with baking paper and lightly spray with canola oil. To make the base, mix all the ingredients together and add a little cold water. Use a butter knife to mix into a dough. Roll out and press lightly into the slice tin. Set aside. To make the cheese sauce topping, beat the egg white with electric beaters for 5 minutes or until tripled in size. Melt the butter with the onion in a small saucepan until the butter is bubbling. Add the flour and mix over low heat. Add the milk, cheese, salt and egg yolk and cook, whisking, until it forms a thick smooth sauce. Remove from the heat and fold in the egg white. Pour the topping over the biscuit base. Bake for 25 minutes, or until golden on top. Serve hot or cold.

Freezing: Allow to cool to room temperature then cut into squares. Wrap in plastic wrap and store on a flat surface. Freeze for up to 2 months.

Thawing: Pop into lunch boxes frozen. Alternatively, allow to sit on the kitchen counter for 5 minutes.

Reheating: If you want the squares warm, microwave for 8–10 seconds on high, or until warm.

Zucchini Slice

I love this recipe. It's great for breakfast, morning tea, lunch, afternoon tea or a light dinner with a garden salad. It freezes well, and is just so easy. Winner!

1 tablespoon butter

1 onion, finely chopped

100 g bacon pieces

400 g zucchini (3–4 medium), grated

¾ cup self-raising flour

½ cup grated cheese

4 eggs, lightly beaten

Preheat the oven to 180°C. Line a shallow baking tin with baking paper. Melt the butter in a frying pan and gently fry the onion until golden. Add the bacon and cook for a couple of minutes. Remove from the heat and cool in the fridge. Place the zucchini in a large mixing bowl and add the cooled onion and bacon mixture, flour and cheese. Mix well. Add the eggs and combine well. Pour the mixture into the baking tin and bake for approximately 30 minutes, or until the top has browned.

Freezing: Allow to cool to room temperature then cut into squares. Wrap in plastic wrap and store on a flat surface. Freeze for up to 2 months.

Thawing: Pop into lunch boxes frozen. Alternatively, allow to sit on the kitchen counter for 5 minutes.

Reheating: If you want the squares warm, microwave for 12–15 seconds on high, or until warm.

Hints & Tips

* When zucchini gets too expensive, try grated pumpkin instead.
* You can also make muffins from this recipe. Use a 12-hole muffin tin lined with paper cases, and bake at 180°C for 20 minutes, or until browned.

Homemade Sausage Rolls

Homemade Sausage Rolls are perfect for so many occasions, from picnics and days out at the beach to birthday parties. In fact, maybe we should say they are perfect for all occasions! This recipe is super easy and incredibly yummy.

500 g sausage mince

½ brown onion, finely diced

1 egg

mixed herbs

1 carrot and/or zucchini, grated

salt and pepper

1 cup breadcrumbs

2 sheets puff pastry

milk, for brushing

Preheat the oven to 200°C. Line a baking tray with baking paper. In a bowl, mix the sausage mince, onion, egg, herbs and vegies together. Season well with salt and pepper. Add the breadcrumbs and mix well. Divide the mince mixture between the sheets of puff pastry, placing along one long edge. Roll the pastry up over the mixture, as though you were rolling sushi. Cut to your desired length and place on the baking tray. Brush with milk. Bake for 25 minutes, or until golden brown.

* *

Freezing: Allow to cool to room temperature then layer on baking paper in an airtight container. Freeze for up to 4 months.

Thawing: Do not thaw; cook from frozen.

Reheating: Place in a preheated oven at 150°C for 15 minutes, or until heated through.

Vegetable and Ham Noodle Cups

Vegetable and Ham Noodle Cups are a fantastic way to get the kids to eat their vegies. Everyone loves noodles and this makes an easy-to-eat-on-the-run snack. Add a salad and you have a complete meal.

olive oil spray

2 × 85 g packets chicken two-minute noodles

3 cups grated vegetables, such as pumpkin, zucchini and carrot

2 eggs, lightly beaten

½ cup light sour cream

½ cup chopped ham

½ cup grated light tasty cheese

Preheat the oven to 180°C. Lightly spray a 12-hole muffin tin with olive oil. Cook the noodles according to the packet instructions, reserving the sachets of flavouring. Drain and rinse under cold water. Place in a bowl and add the flavouring (I usually just use one, but it's up to you), vegetables, eggs, sour cream and ham. Divide between the holes in the muffin tin and top with cheese. Bake for 30–35 minutes, or until set.

* *

Freezing: Allow to cool to room temperature then layer on baking paper in an airtight container. Freeze for up to 1 month.

Thawing: Do not thaw; cook from frozen.

Reheating: Pan fry until heated through, or place in a preheated oven at 200°C for 5 minutes. (Don't microwave or they will go soggy.)

Hints & Tips

* You can substitute mayonnaise for the sour cream.
* Leftover pasta is a good substitute for the two-minute noodles.

Mini Quiches

Mini Quiches are an all-time favourite. These freeze really well and are perfect for when guests drop by, for kids' lunches, or just as a snack.

24 slices fresh bread, crusts removed

butter, for spreading

4 eggs, beaten

1 cup milk

½ cup cream or Greek yoghurt

4 rashers bacon, rind removed, chopped

1 brown onion, finely chopped

1 cup grated cheese

Preheat the oven to 180°C. Grease two 12-hole muffin tins. Butter the bread and press firmly (butter side down) into the holes in the muffin tins. Bake for 10 minutes then remove from the oven but leave in the tins. Whisk the eggs, milk and cream or yoghurt together in a jug. Fry the bacon and onion until just starting to brown and divide between the bread 'cups'. Pour the egg mixture over the top and sprinkle with cheese. Bake for 30 minutes, or until golden and puffed.

* *

Freezing: Allow to cool to room temperature then layer on baking paper in an airtight container. Freeze for up to 1 month.

Thawing: Pop into lunch boxes frozen. Alternatively, allow to sit on the kitchen counter for 5 minutes.

Reheating: If you want the quiches warm, microwave for 8–10 seconds on high, or until warm.

Hints & Tips

* Add extra ingredients such as chopped spinach, diced cherry tomatoes, grated zucchini or carrot.

Lasagne Cups

These Lasagne Cups are perfect freezer food. Make individual serves and pop one in the oven for lunch or frozen into a lunch box.

canola oil spray

1 tablespoon olive oil

1 brown onion, finely diced

1 clove garlic, crushed

500 g beef or chicken mince

1 × 420 g can tomato soup (or 1 × 410 g can crushed tomatoes and 1 tablespoon tomato paste)

24 wonton wrappers

1 cup ricotta cheese

½ cup grated cheddar cheese

Preheat the oven to 180°C. Spray a 12-hole muffin tin liberally with canola oil. Heat the olive oil in a saucepan and brown the onion and garlic. Add the mince and brown well. Add the tomato soup and simmer for 15 minutes, or until thickened. Set aside. Place a wonton wrapper in each hole in the muffin tin and push down to the bottom. Divide half the ricotta cheese between the holes. Do the same with half the bolognaise sauce, then add another wonton wrapper, pressing over the mixture quite firmly. Repeat with the remaining ricotta cheese and bolognaise sauce. Top with the cheese and bake in the oven for 15–20 minutes, or until cooked through and golden. Allow the lasagne cups to cool slightly in the tin before removing. Serve hot or cold.

Freezing: Allow to cool to room temperature then layer on baking paper in an airtight container. Freeze for up to 5 months.

Thawing: Pop into lunch boxes frozen. Alternatively, allow to sit in the fridge overnight.

Reheating: Place in a preheated oven at 150°C for 15 minutes, or until heated through.

Garlic Bread

Homemade Garlic Bread is very simple and tastes delightful. It only takes a few minutes to prepare and cook. Makes your dinner stretch that little bit further for less!

200 g butter, softened

2 cloves garlic, crushed

½ cup grated parmesan cheese

2 Turkish bread loaves

Preheat the oven to 200°C. In a small bowl mix together the butter, garlic and parmesan until well combined. Take the Turkish breads out of their packets and slice into 1.5-cm slices – a typical loaf should get you about 10–12 slices. Butter one side of the bread, making sure you go right to the edges, using all the mixture. If baking immediately, place butter side up on a lined baking tray and bake for 12 minutes.

Freezing: Layer the uncooked bread on baking paper in an airtight container. Loosely cover with baking paper before sealing. Freeze for up to 2 months.

Thawing: Allow to sit in the fridge for 4–5 hours or on the kitchen counter for 1 hour.

Reheating: Place in a preheated oven at 200°C for 12 minutes, or until golden brown.

Chicken and Apple Sausages

Chicken and Apple Sausages is a great one for the kids to make and eat –
especially over the school holidays.

125 g chicken breast

½ apple, cored and peeled

2 tablespoons breadcrumbs, plus extra for coating

2 tablespoons grated parmesan cheese

1 tablespoon chopped fresh parsley

vegetable oil, for frying

Place the chicken, apple, breadcrumbs, parmesan and parsley into a food processor. Process until finely minced and mixed. Roll tablespoonfuls into small sausages (about 1 centimetre thick and 4 centimetres long). The mixture will be very sticky. Refrigerate on a plate for an hour. Roll the chilled sausages in breadcrumbs. Shallow fry in vegetable oil until golden.

Freezing: Allow to cool to room temperature then layer on baking paper in an airtight container. Freeze for up to 4 months.

Thawing: Allow to sit in the fridge overnight or on the kitchen counter for 30 minutes, covered by a tea towel.

Reheating: Place in a preheated oven at 150°C for 15 minutes, or until heated through.

Desserts

It's always good to have
a few desserts pre-frozen
in your freezer for the nights
you need something sweet. Most of
these are non-cooked ice-cream based
desserts, so you just whip them together
and freeze until needed – easy! A few
make for wonderfully easy birthday
or celebration dishes too.

Watermelon Bombe

Watermelon Bombe is one of my favourite 'cakes' to make for my children on their birthdays. It can be a bit fiddly, but the wow factor is certainly worth the time and effort.

1 litre vanilla ice-cream

green food colouring

peppermint essence

400 ml cream

100 g chocolate drops

500 ml strawberry
ice-cream

Line a round deep bowl with plastic wrap. Place the vanilla ice-cream into a food processor with enough green colouring to make it watermelon-rind colour and a capful of peppermint essence. Mix until well combined. Spread over the bottom and sides of the bowl and place in the freezer until well set. For the 'pith' layer, whip the cream and layer this on top of the green ice-cream layer. Place in the freezer to set. Mix the chocolate drops through the strawberry ice-cream and fill the bowl to the top. Add another layer of plastic wrap. Freeze overnight.

* *

Freezing: Leave in the container and cover with plastic wrap with the plastic touching the ice-cream (to prevent water crystals forming). Freeze for up to 4 months.

Thawing: Serve frozen but remove from the freezer 10 minutes before serving to soften enough to remove from the bowl. Turn onto a plate and serve immediately.

Hints & Tips

* When serving the watermelon bombe, flip it over, and take out a slice to show your audience the frozen watermelon – including seeds!

Raspberry and Malteser Ice-cream Cake

Raspberry and Malteser Ice-cream Cake is such a yummy dessert – cheap and so easy to make! Adjust the amount of Maltesers and raspberries to your taste (but don't put too many raspberries in it because their flavour can be quite overpowering).

1 litre vanilla ice-cream

1½ × 155 g bags Maltesers

1½ cups frozen raspberries, plus extra to serve

Soften the ice-cream slightly either by leaving it out of the freezer for a little while or by microwaving for 30 seconds at a time. Line a round cake tin with plastic wrap and cover the bottom with a layer of Maltesers. Roughly crush the remaining Maltesers and stir through the ice-cream along with the raspberries. Pour into the cake tin and cover with plastic wrap (touching the ice-cream to prevent any freezer burn). Freeze overnight. Cut into slices and serve with a few raspberries scattered over the top.

* *

Freezing: Leave in the container and cover with plastic wrap with the plastic touching the ice-cream (to prevent water crystals forming). Freeze for up to 4 months.

Thawing: Serve frozen but remove from the freezer 10 minutes before serving to soften enough to remove from the tin. Turn onto a plate and serve immediately.

Deep-fried Ice-cream

I remember my dad taking me to the local Chinese restaurant in Belmont, Perth, for the best Deep-fried Ice-cream I've ever had. The servings were just enormous and came with a decadent caramel sauce. My version is much smaller, but I always keep a few of the balls in the freezer for a super fast dessert, as all the work is in the preparation!

1 litre full-cream vanilla ice-cream (low-fat won't work here)

1 cup shredded coconut

½ cup breadcrumbs

1 teaspoon nutmeg

2 tablespoons brown sugar

1 egg

½ cup milk

canola oil, for frying

Freeze a metal baking tray for 1 hour. Lay out a piece of plastic wrap on the bench and scoop enough ice-cream into the plastic wrap to roughly make a ball 5 centimetres across. Gather up the plastic wrap around the ice-cream (so your hands aren't touching the ice-cream) and quickly form a rough ball shape. Place the ball in the plastic wrap on the cold baking tray, and place in the freezer. Repeat until you have run out of ice-cream. The number you make will depend on the size of the balls – but no smaller than 5 centimetres across. Freeze the balls for at least an hour. Then one by one, take out the balls (still in their wrap) and 'roll' them on the counter to get more of a perfect ball shape. When you're happy with the shape, return to the freezer and leave for another hour. In a small bowl, mix together the coconut, breadcrumbs, nutmeg and sugar. Take out one ball at a time, hold in your hand for about 20 seconds to soften the outer layer, then remove from the plastic wrap and roll the ball in the coconut mixture to cover it all over.

Return the ball to the plastic wrap and return to the freezer. Again, do this for all the balls, using half the coconut mixture. Freeze for at least half an hour. In another bowl mix the egg and milk together, take the balls out, roll in the egg wash mixture, and then roll in the remaining coconut mixture. Wrap in plastic wrap and freeze until needed. In a small saucepan, heat the canola oil until it is hot enough to brown a small piece of bread in 15 seconds. Carefully place the balls one at a time into the oil to cook the outside. This only takes about 30 seconds. Remove and drain on paper towel.

Freezing: Wrap coated (but uncooked) balls individually in plastic wrap. Freeze for up to 4 months.

Thawing: Do not thaw; cook from frozen.

Reheating: Cook as above.

After-dinner Mint Ice-cream Slice

You know those yummy after-dinner mints? Well, this is a delicious After-dinner Mint Ice-cream Slice – creamy smooth with the crunch of chocolate and mint through it!

250 ml thickened cream

300 ml cooking cream

5 Peppermint Crisp bars

250 g chocolate biscuits (rectangular or round)

Beat the thickened cream until firm. Add the cooking cream and beat until just thick again. You don't want to overbeat, as the cream will start to separate. Crush four of the Peppermint Crisp bars into chunks and stir through the cream mixture. Line a square cake tin (or round if using round biscuits) with baking paper or plastic wrap. Ensure the paper hangs over the edges so you can use it to lift out the slice once set. Place the biscuits in the base of the tin and pour cream mix on top. Cover with plastic wrap and freeze overnight. When set crush the remaining Peppermint Crisp and sprinkle on top, then cut and serve immediately.

Freezing: Leave in the container and cover with plastic wrap with the plastic touching the ice-cream (to prevent water crystals forming). Freeze for up to 4 months.

Thawing: Serve frozen but remove from the freezer 10 minutes before serving to soften enough to remove from the tin. Turn onto a plate and serve immediately.

Teacup-baked Cheesecakes

A lovely way to serve your dessert. If you're worried about your teacups,
place them in a baking dish and add a bit of water to create a water bath.

1 tablespoon syrup
(any sort – golden,
maple, etc.)

6 butternut biscuits

250 g cream cheese

2 eggs

½ cup milk

½ cup white sugar

1 teaspoon vanilla
extract

cream or ice-cream,
to serve

Preheat the oven to 160°C. Place six teacups on a baking tray. Put a tiny dollop of syrup in the bottom of each teacup and place a butternut biscuit on top (the syrup is to hold the biscuit down during cooking). In a food processor, blend the cream cheese, eggs, milk, sugar and vanilla together until smooth. Divide the mixture between the teacups, leaving a good 1.5-centimetre gap at the top to allow the cheesecakes to rise. Cook for 25 minutes, or until the top starts rising and browns slightly. Turn off the oven and leave the cheesecakes inside for 20 minutes. Serve on a saucer with some cream or ice-cream.

Freezing: Leave in the teacups and allow to cool then cover with plastic wrap with the plastic touching the cheesecake (to prevent water crystals forming). Freeze for up to 4 months.

Thawing: Allow to sit on the kitchen counter for 10–15 minutes.

Reheating: Microwave for 20 seconds or place in a preheated oven at 150°C for 15 minutes.

Frozen Strawberry Cheesecake Slice

This slice is an explosion of flavours so you only need a little bit to feel satisfied! Cut into thin slices and serve with Chantilly cream or fruit salad.

BASE

canola oil spray

2 cups crushed Scotch Finger biscuits

½ cup Nutella

1 tablespoon butter

FILLING

250 g cream cheese

180 ml thickened cream

½ cup raspberry cordial

250 g strawberries, chopped

Line the base of a springform cake tin with baking paper and spray liberally with canola oil. In a food processor, mix the Scotch Finger biscuits, Nutella and butter until a slightly sticky crumb forms. Pour into the cake tin and press firmly and evenly into the bottom. Using electric beaters, mix together the cream cheese and cream until smooth (about 3 minutes). Add the raspberry cordial and mix until the colour is even. Fold the strawberries into the mixture then pour over the biscuit base. Cover with plastic wrap (just touching the slice) and freeze until just firm (about 4 hours). Slice into wedges to serve.

* *

Freezing: Leave in the container and cover with plastic wrap with the plastic touching the slice (to prevent water crystals forming). Freeze for up to 4 months.

Thawing: Serve frozen but remove from the freezer 10 minutes before serving to soften enough to remove from the tin. Turn onto a plate and serve immediately.

Hints & Tips

* Raspberries, blueberries or bananas can be substituted for the strawberries.

Apple Turnovers

This recipe makes eight turnovers, and they taste superb! So sweet and delicious. Serve with ice-cream, cream or custard.

2 sheets puff pastry, thawed

1 × 400 g can pie apple

2 tablespoons brown sugar

½ teaspoon cinnamon

milk, for brushing

white sugar, for decorating (optional)

Preheat the oven to 200°C. Line a large baking tray with baking paper. Using a sharp knife, cut the two sheets of pastry into quarters. Pour the pie apple into a bowl and combine with the brown sugar and cinnamon. Mix well. Divide the mixture evenly into the centre of the eight pastry squares. Brush the corners of the squares with milk and fold over so that the contents are enclosed in triangles. Use a fork to seal the edges. Brush milk over the triangles, and if you wish, sprinkle with a little white sugar. Bake for 20–25 minutes or until golden.

* *

Freezing: Wrap individual uncooked turnovers in plastic wrap. Freeze for up to 6 weeks.

Thawing: Do not thaw; cook from frozen.

Reheating: Cook as above.

Chocolate Ravioli

You can use any type of chocolate bar for this recipe – I've used Snickers here, but any milk or white chocolate is also fantastic. Dessert is only 10 minutes away. So naughty it needs a good smack!

1 sheet puff pastry

1 × 60 g Snickers bar

milk, for brushing

icing sugar, for dusting

vanilla ice-cream,
to serve

Preheat the oven to 200°C. Line a tray with baking paper. With a sharp knife, cut the pastry into 16 even squares. Cut the Snickers bar into eight even pieces (it helps to refrigerate it first – and use a very sharp knife). Place a piece of Snickers in the centre of a piece of pastry, use the milk to moisten around the chocolate and place another square of pastry on top. Use a fork to seal the edges the whole way around. Repeat with the remaining pastry and Snickers pieces. Bake for 10–12 minutes or until the pastry is golden and puffed. Dust with icing sugar and serve with vanilla ice-cream.

* *

Freezing: Chocolate Ravioli should be frozen uncooked, individually wrapped in plastic wrap for up to 6 weeks.

Thawing: Do not thaw; cook from frozen.

Reheating: Place in a preheated oven at 180°C for 20 minutes, or until the pastry is golden.

Sticky Date Caramel Slab

Oh my, this is a keeper. Deliciously sweet and goes really well with either ice-cream or cream.

2 cups chopped dates

1 cup water

100 g butter

⅓ cup brown sugar

¼ cup maple syrup

1 teaspoon bicarbonate of soda

1 teaspoon minced ginger

2 cups self-raising flour

2 teaspoons cinnamon

3 eggs, lightly beaten

CARAMEL ICING

¼ cup brown sugar

40 g butter

2 tablespoons sour cream

1 cup icing sugar, sifted

1 teaspoon vanilla essence

Preheat the oven to 180°C. Line a lamington tray with baking paper. Place the dates and water in a saucepan and bring to the boil. Add the butter, brown sugar and maple syrup and return to the boil. Add the bicarbonate of soda and minced ginger and mix. Remove from the heat and allow to cool slightly. Sift the flour and cinnamon together into a large bowl. Add the eggs and mix well. Stir in the date mixture with a wooden spoon until smooth. Pour into the lamington tray and bake for 25 minutes. To make the icing, heat the brown sugar and butter together in a saucepan over medium heat until the butter has melted. Remove from the heat and stir in the sour cream, icing sugar and vanilla. Whisk until smooth. Allow both the cake and icing to cool before pouring the icing over the cake.

Freezing: Wrap individual slices in plastic wrap and store flat. Freeze for up to 4 months.

Thawing: Allow to sit on the kitchen counter for 10–15 minutes.

Reheating: Microwave for 20 seconds or place in a preheated oven at 150°C for 15 minutes.

Biscuits and Slices

Ahhh, biscuits
… they truly are my
weakness. Once I sit down at
night after the kids have gone to bed,
with my hot cup of tea, I must have a
biscuit or my night is not complete. Here
is a selection of my personal favourites.
The Peanut Butter Biscuits would be
my all-time favourite – and I've
been making that recipe
since I was 10!

120 Biscuits for $7

Looking for a bulk biscuit recipe? Well, this one is for you. It makes up to 120 biscuits for just less than 7 dollars! This fantastic basic recipe is terrific value and has lots of room for variations. Now you'll always have fresh biscuits only 10 minutes away.

500 g butter or margarine

1 cup sugar

1 × 395 g can sweetened condensed milk

5 cups self-raising flour, sifted

Preheat the oven to 180°C. Line a baking tray with baking paper. Cream the butter or margarine and sugar together until light and fluffy. Add the condensed milk and self-raising flour and mix to form a dough. Add the flavourings of your choice (see opposite). Roll into teaspoon-sized balls and press down with a fork (dip the fork in flour first so it doesn't stick). Place on the baking tray and bake until golden brown (approximately 10–15 minutes). For a less 'floury' biscuit, substitute half a cup of custard powder for half a cup of the flour.

Freezing: Can be frozen in dough form or biscuit form. To freeze the dough, roll into a long 'sausage' approximately 3 centimetres thick. Wrap the sausage in baking paper, then plastic wrap. Freeze for up to 2 months. To freeze the cooked biscuits, cool to room temperature before placing in a ziplock bag. Freeze for up to 6 weeks.

Thawing: Do not thaw the frozen dough (see reheating instructions below). To thaw the cooked biscuits, allow to sit on the kitchen counter for 5 minutes.

Reheating: Cut the dough into 'coins' straight from the frozen dough. Place on a baking tray and follow the cooking instructions. Cooked biscuits do not need to be reheated.

These are some suggested variations:

* Chocolate chip (milk or white)
* Corn flakes and sultanas
* Hundreds and thousands
* Malted milk
* Milo and coconut
* Peanut butter
* Jam drops
* Dried apricot with ginger and rolled in coconut
* Chocolate with ginger
* White chocolate and macadamia nuts
* Sultanas and orange zest

Hints & Tips

* For a healthier version, substitute an egg for half the butter.
* If you wish to use cookie cutters, add more flour to make the dough stiffer.
* Try sandwiching two together with custard icing.
* Dip the uncooked dough into raw sugar coloured with food colouring.

Sweetened Condensed Milk Substitute

If you have run out of cans of condensed milk, here is a 'from scratch' version for you to try:

2 eggs

1 cup brown sugar

1 teaspoon vanilla essence

2 tablespoons flour

½ teaspoon baking powder

¼ teaspoon salt

Mix all the ingredients together and use as a substitute for sweetened condensed milk in recipes for pies, balls and desserts, such as Chocolate Condensed Milk Balls (page 179).

Old-fashioned Corn-flake Biscuits

Remember having these delicious biscuits as a kid? My grandma made the best version in the whole world – this is her recipe.

125 g butter

⅔ cup brown sugar

1 teaspoon vanilla extract

2 eggs

1¾ cups self-raising flour, sifted

1 cup sultanas

1½ cups corn flakes, lightly crushed

Preheat the oven to 180°C. Line two baking trays with baking paper. Use an electric beater to beat together the butter, sugar and vanilla in a large bowl until pale and creamy. Add the eggs, one at a time, beating well after each addition until combined. Fold in the flour and sultanas until combined. Place the corn flakes on a plate. Use your hands to roll tablespoonfuls of the cookie mixture into biscuit shapes, press them into the corn flakes and place on the baking trays. Cook for 18–20 minutes, or until golden, swapping the position of the trays in the oven halfway through cooking. Remove from the oven and set aside on the trays for 5 minutes before transferring to a wire rack to cool completely.

Freezing: Allow to cool to room temperature then place into ziplock bags. Freeze for up to 2 months. Don't freeze as dough as the corn flakes will tend to go rubbery.

Thawing: Allow to sit on the kitchen counter for 5 minutes.

Hints & Tips

* Chocolate chips can be substituted for the sultanas.
* Dried cranberries and pepitas make for delicious alternatives to the sultanas and corn flakes.

Nana Darling Jam Drops

This is my Nana Darling's recipe, these jam drops are light, fluffy, and that gooey jam centre ... oh boy!

110 g butter

¾ cup sugar

2 eggs

½ cup cornflour

1¾ cups self-raising flour

½ cup strawberry jam

Preheat the oven to 180°C. Line a baking tray with baking paper. Cream the butter and sugar together using an electric mixer. Add the eggs and beat until fluffy. Sift the cornflour and self-raising flour together and add to the creamed butter mixture. Beat until just combined. Lightly flour your hands (the mix will be slightly sticky to touch but this is the perfect consistency). Roll heaped teaspoonfuls of the mixture into balls and place on the baking tray. Push a hole in the centre of each ball using your finger. Add 1 teaspoon of jam to each centre hole. Bake for 8–10 minutes, until just turning golden brown.

Freezing: Allow to cool to room temperature then place in ziplock bags. Freeze for up to 2 months. The dough can be frozen (without the jam, of course) the same way, if you should wish.

Thawing: To thaw the cooked biscuits, allow to sit on the kitchen counter for 5 minutes.

Hints & Tips

* Can be made with any flavour of jam your tastebuds prefer.
* Store in an airtight container for up to 2 weeks.

Peanut Butter Biscuits

This recipe for Peanut Butter Biscuits has been in my family for years. They never last long in our house! We also have a gluten-free version opposite.

140 g plain flour

½ teaspoon bicarbonate of soda

½ teaspoon salt

115 g butter

165 g brown sugar

1 egg

1 teaspoon vanilla extract

265 g crunchy peanut butter

Preheat the oven to 180°C. Line two baking trays with baking paper. Sift together the flour, bicarbonate of soda and salt and set aside. In a food processor, cream the butter and sugar together until light and fluffy. Add the egg and vanilla and mix well. Add the peanut butter a spoonful at a time. Remove the wet mixture and transfer to a large bowl. Fold in the dry ingredients and refrigerate for 30 minutes. Roll rounded teaspoonfuls of the mixture into balls and place on the baking trays. Flatten them slightly with your hand, then press lightly with a fork dipped in flour one way then the opposite way to get a diamond effect. Cook for 12–15 minutes until golden.

Freezing: Can be frozen in dough form or biscuit form. To freeze the dough, roll into a long 'sausage' approximately 3 centimetres thick. Wrap sausage in baking paper, then plastic wrap. Freeze for up to 2 months. To freeze the cooked biscuits, cool to room temperature before placing in a ziplock bag. Freeze for up to 6 weeks.

Thawing: Do not thaw the frozen cookie dough (see reheating instructions below). To thaw the cooked biscuits, allow to sit on the kitchen counter for 5 minutes.

Reheating: Cut the frozen dough into 'coins'. Place on a baking tray and follow the cooking instructions. Cooked biscuits do not need to be reheated.

Gluten-free Peanut Butter Biscuits

1 cup crunchy peanut butter

1 cup brown sugar

1 egg

pinch of bicarbonate of soda

½ cup (or more!) chocolate chips (I use the tiny ones)

Preheat the oven to 160°C. Line two baking trays with baking paper. Mix the peanut butter, sugar, egg and bicarbonate of soda together, then fold in the chocolate chips. Place small blobs on the baking trays well spaced apart (they really spread, I get 25–30 out of this – use more trays or cook in batches if necessary). Bake for 8–10 minutes, or until golden. Keep a careful eye on them that they don't brown too much. When you take them out they should still be very soft – you will think they are underdone – but they harden as they cool. Besides, even if they are slightly 'undercooked' they are very nice when gooey!

* *

For other gluten-free recipes see:

* Gluten-free White Chocolate Cake – page 201
* Gluten-free Almond and Raspberry Cake – page 202
* Gluten-free Banana Bread – page 203

Custard Creams

I remember camping as a child and Mum had made a huge batch of custard cream biscuits for us to enjoy. They were buttery and melt-in-the-mouth, and they didn't last long. Now you can enjoy them too!

BISCUITS

185 g butter

½ cup caster sugar

2 eggs

2 cups self-raising flour, sifted

½ cup custard powder, sifted

FILLING

125 g butter

1 cup icing sugar, plus extra for dusting

2 tablespoons custard powder

1 teaspoon orange zest

2 teaspoons orange juice

Preheat the oven to 180°C. Line a baking tray with baking paper. To make the biscuits, cream the butter and sugar together until light and fluffy. Gradually beat in the eggs, mixing well after each addition. Gradually fold in the flour and custard powder. Place teaspoonfuls of the mixture on the tray and squash down with a fork. Bake for 10–12 minutes. Cool the biscuits on a wire rack.

To make the filling, cream the butter, icing sugar and custard powder together until light and fluffy. Add the orange zest and juice and beat until combined. Spread the flat side of one biscuit with filling, sandwich together with another and dust with icing sugar.

✳ ✳

Freezing: Can be frozen in dough form or biscuit form. To freeze the dough, roll into a ball, wrap in baking paper, then in plastic wrap. Freeze for up to 2 months. To freeze the cooked biscuits, cool to room temperature before placing in a ziplock bag. Freeze for up to 6 weeks.

Thawing: Allow the dough to thaw overnight in the fridge, then follow the cooking instructions. To thaw the cooked biscuits, allow to sit on the kitchen counter for 5 minutes before icing.

Hints & Tips

✳ Can be kept in an airtight container for up to a week.

Jody's Chewy Biscuits

These biscuits are just divine – sweet, chewy and crunchy, with the perfect ratio of chocolate to biscuit.

1 cup unsalted butter

½ cup light brown sugar, firmly packed

½ cup dark brown sugar, firmly packed

1 cup caster sugar

1 tablespoon vanilla extract

1 egg

2 ½ cups plain white flour

1 teaspoon baking powder

¾ teaspoon salt

2 ½ cups chocolate chips

Preheat the oven to 180°C. Line two baking trays with baking paper. Cream the butter with the sugars until well blended. Stir in the vanilla extract and add the egg. Sift together the flour, baking powder and salt and fold into the mixture. Add the chocolate chips of your choice. Gather the dough into a loose ball, cover with plastic wrap and place in the fridge for at least an hour. Form into rounds the size of a golf ball and place 3 centimetres apart on the baking trays. Bake until just light brown around the edges (14–16 minutes). Too much cooking will make the biscuits hard. Cool on a wire rack. Initially they may seem a little underdone, but they will firm up as they cool.

Freezing: Can be frozen in dough form or biscuit form. To freeze the dough, roll into a ball, wrap in baking paper, then in plastic wrap. Freeze for up to 2 months. To freeze the cooked biscuits, cool to room temperature before placing in a ziplock bag. Freeze for up to 6 weeks.

Thawing: Do not thaw the frozen cookie dough (see reheating instructions below). To thaw the cooked biscuits, allow to sit on the kitchen counter for 5 minutes.

Reheating: Cut the frozen dough into 'coins'. Place on a baking tray and follow the cooking instructions. Cooked biscuits do not need to be reheated.

Monte Carlos

*Homemade Monte Carlos beat shop-bought ones any day! They're fun,
easy to make and taste delightful. You can make them for any occasion.*

BISCUITS

185 g butter

½ cup caster sugar

1 egg

1 teaspoon vanilla
extract

1¼ cups self-raising
flour

½ cup desiccated
coconut

FILLING

60 g butter

¾ cup icing sugar

½ teaspoon vanilla
extract

2 teaspoons milk

raspberry jam, for filling

Preheat the oven to 180°C. Lightly grease a
baking tray or line with baking paper. To make
the biscuits, cream the butter and sugar together
until light and fluffy. Add the egg and vanilla
extract and beat well. Sift the flour and add
the coconut, then fold into the mixture. Roll
teaspoons of the mixture into balls and place on
the baking tray. Press down lightly with a fork.
Try to keep all the biscuits a uniform size. Bake
for 10–12 minutes, or until golden. Remove and
cool on a wire rack. To make the filling, cream
the butter and icing sugar together until light and
fluffy. Add the vanilla and then gradually add the
milk, beating well. To assemble the biscuits, put
a teaspoon of jam on the bottom of one biscuit
and a teaspoon of the cream filling on another.
Sandwich together with a slight twist.

Freezing: Can be frozen in dough form or biscuit
form. To freeze the dough, roll into a ball, wrap in
baking paper, then in plastic wrap. Freeze for up
to 2 months. To freeze the cooked biscuits, cool to
room temperature before placing in a ziplock bag.
Freeze for up to 6 weeks.

Thawing: Allow the dough to thaw overnight
in the fridge, then follow cooking instructions.
To thaw the cooked biscuits, allow to sit on the
kitchen counter for 5 minutes before icing.

Clinker Slice

Hands up if you love Clinkers! Even now I still close my eyes and try to guess what colour I've got after taking a bite. This Clinker Slice recipe combines the best of slice with Clinkers – what more could you ask for?

250 g Malt 'o' Milk biscuits

200 g Clinkers

125 g butter

1 cup sweetened condensed milk

200 g milk chocolate buttons

Place the biscuits and Clinkers in a food processor and blend into small chunky pieces. In a small saucepan over low heat, cook the butter and condensed milk, stirring constantly for 2 minutes, or until the butter is melted. Remove from the heat and pour straight into the Clinker mix and stir through until well coated. Line a slice tin with baking paper and press the Clinker mix into the tin. Melt the chocolate buttons in a bowl in the microwave for 30 seconds then stir. If they are not all melted, microwave for 15 seconds and stir again. Repeat until the chocolate has all melted. Pour the chocolate over the Clinker mix and spread evenly using the back of a metal spoon. Place in the fridge for 2 hours to set. Slice into squares and serve.

Freezing: Line an airtight container with baking paper. Place the slices on the baking paper, add another piece on top and seal well. Freeze for up to 1 month.

Thawing: Allow to sit on the kitchen counter for 5 minutes.

Mars Bar Slice

Mars Bar Slice is a deliciously mouth-watering and decadent slice – just looking at them makes me salivate. This slice takes around 10 minutes to prepare and 3 hours to set.

4 × 65 g Mars Bars, chopped

155 g butter

4 cups Rice Bubbles

200 g milk chocolate

Melt the Mars Bars and 125 grams of the butter together in a heavy-based saucepan over low heat. When melted, add the Rice Bubbles and combine. Press the mixture into a lined slice tin and refrigerate for about 3 hours, or until set. For the topping, melt the chocolate and remaining butter together in the microwave, stir until smooth and spread over the base. Leave until set.

Freezing: Line an airtight container with baking paper. Place the slices on the baking paper, add another piece on top and seal well. Freeze for up to 1 month.

Thawing: Allow to sit on the kitchen counter for 5 minutes.

* Mars Bar Slice can be kept in a sealed airtight container in the fridge for up to a week.

Frugal Chocolate Slice

This Frugal Chocolate Slice is a basic, tasty treat. Perfect for the school lunch box or a snack in the cookie jar!

1 cup self-raising flour

¾ cup brown sugar

1 tablespoon cocoa

1 cup Rice Bubbles

125 g butter

icing sugar, to dust

Preheat the oven to 180°C. Line a slice tin with baking paper. Combine the flour, sugar, cocoa and Rice Bubbles in a mixing bowl. Melt the butter over low heat and pour into the mixture. Mix well. Press into the slice tin, then bake for 10 minutes. Dust with icing sugar.

Freezing: Layer an airtight container with baking paper. Place the slice on the baking paper, add another piece on top and seal well. Freeze for up to 1 month.

Thawing: Allow to sit on the kitchen counter for 5 minutes.

Hints & Tips

✶ You can sprinkle with desiccated coconut instead of icing sugar, if you prefer.

Chocolate Chickpea Slice

This probably sounds a bit weird, but it is so delicious! It's high in protein, thanks to the chickpeas, so a tiny piece goes a long way to filling you up. You can adjust the sweetness, according to taste, simply by modifying the amounts of honey and cocoa (more honey or less cocoa = sweeter, more cocoa or less honey = less sweet).

1 cup milk chocolate, chopped

1 × 400 g can chickpeas, drained and rinsed

¼ cup natural yoghurt

2 tablespoons cocoa

⅓ cup honey

¼ cup pecans

¼ cup shredded coconut

3 eggs

Preheat the oven to 180°C. Line a slice tin with baking paper. Melt the chocolate in a glass bowl placed over a pot of simmering water. While the chocolate is melting, process the chickpeas in a food processor (you can chop the chickpeas as finely or coarsely as you like). Add the yoghurt, cocoa, honey, pecans, coconut and eggs. Process until just combined. Add the mixture to the melted chocolate and mix until well combined. Pour into the slice tin and bake for 25–30 minutes or until the mixture is just set. Allow to cool completely then cut into pieces.

Freezing: Line an airtight container with baking paper. Place the slice on the baking paper, add another piece on top and seal well. Freeze for up to 1 month.

Thawing: Allow to sit on the kitchen counter for 5 minutes.

Lemon Lunch Box Slice

I am always on the lookout for snack ideas, and this slice went down a treat in the kids' school lunch boxes.

125 g butter

165 g plain flour

½ cup icing sugar

TOPPING

2 eggs, lightly beaten

1 cup caster sugar

4 teaspoons lemon juice

1 teaspoon finely grated lemon zest

Preheat the oven to 180°C. Beat the butter, 150 grams of the flour and the icing sugar together until they form a soft dough. Put the dough on a lightly floured surface and knead briefly. Press the dough into a shallow rectangular slice tin and bake for 20 minutes. Allow to cool in the tin. To make the topping, combine the eggs, caster sugar, remaining flour, lemon juice and zest in a bowl and mix until combined. Pour over the cooked base and cook for 25–30 minutes, or until firm. Place in the fridge until cold, then cut into slices.

* *

Freezing: Line an airtight container with baking paper. Place the slice on the baking paper, add another piece on top and seal well. Freeze for up to 1 month.

Thawing: Allow to sit on the kitchen counter for 5 minutes.

Hints & Tips

* Dust with icing sugar just before serving.
* You can substitute lime juice for the lemon juice.

Chocolate Cheesecake Brownie Muffins

I first tried this recipe about 10 years ago when attempting to use up some Easter eggs I still had lying around. It is a very rich and heavy muffin, so would make a great dessert if served warm with ice-cream.

CHEESECAKE

250 g cream cheese

½ cup caster sugar

1 teaspoon vanilla essence

2 eggs, beaten

¼ cup plain flour

CHOCOLATE

190 g milk chocolate, chopped

160 g butter, cubed

¾ cup brown sugar

3 eggs, beaten

¾ cup plain flour

Preheat the oven to 180°C. Use butter to grease a 12-hole standard muffin tin. Whip the cream cheese and caster sugar together until smooth. Stir in the vanilla essence and the eggs. Add the flour. Mix until smooth and put aside until ready for use. For the chocolate mixture, melt the chocolate and butter in a bowl in the microwave on low power, stirring every minute for 1–2 minutes until completely melted. Cool slightly. Add the sugar and eggs, and mix well. Stir in the flour until well combined. Divide the chocolate mixture over the 12 muffin holes, then spoon the cheesecake mixture over the top. Get a skewer and gently swirl the mixture so it 'marbles'. Cook for 25 minutes or until a skewer inserted into the centre comes out only slightly gooey (you don't want it cooked perfectly all the way though – you want a bit of goo in the middle).

* *
*

Freezing: Line an airtight container with baking paper. Place the muffins on the baking paper, add another piece on top and seal well. Freeze for up to 1 month.

Thawing: Allow to sit on the kitchen counter for 5 minutes.

Hints & Tips ✳

* These muffins don't rise up high like normal muffins – they only rise a little bit!

* Serve with chocolate icing (to be extra, extra evil) – or just fresh whipped cream and perhaps some strawberries.

Raw Date Squares

If you're trying to eat better and want a guilt-free snack, try our Raw Date Squares. Naturally sweet, they have no added sugar.

1½ cups dates

1 cup desiccated coconut

1½ cups mixed nuts

2 tablespoons coconut oil

¼ cup dried apricots

Place all the ingredients into a food processor and blend until dark and well combined (approximately 4–5 minutes). Press into a lined slice tin and refrigerate for 2–3 hours, until set. Cut into squares. Keep covered in the fridge for up to a week.

Freezing: Line an airtight container with baking paper. Place the squares on the baking paper, add another piece on top and seal well. Freeze for up to 1 month.

Thawing: Allow to sit on the kitchen counter for 5 minutes.

Hints & Tips

* Raw Date Squares are best eaten cold from the fridge. If they are allowed to stand at room temperature for more than 20 minutes they start to soften.
* You can substitute almond meal for the mixed nuts.

Coconut Cream Balls 176

Apricot Balls 177

Cherry Ripe Cheesecake Balls 178

Chocolate Condensed Milk Balls 179

Milo Balls 180

Tim Tam Balls 181

Balls

Balls – small, round and easy to pop into your mouth. They are excellent little bites for parties, barbecues and celebrations. And kids love getting involved making them, too. Remember, when rolling your balls, damp hands make them much easier to handle.

Coconut Cream Balls

Coconut Cream Balls make a great addition to any table. Best of all they freeze really well. Made with coconut cream and white chocolate, they are a gourmet bite of deliciousness!

½ cup coconut cream

1 cup shredded coconut

220 g white chocolate, chopped

1 tablespoon butter

In a medium saucepan, bring the coconut cream and three-quarters of the shredded coconut to a simmer. Remove from the heat and stir in the chocolate until melted, then set aside for about 5 minutes. Add the butter and stir to combine. Cover and refrigerate for at least 3 hours. Roll the mixture into balls and coat with the remaining coconut. Chill in the fridge for at least 2–3 hours before serving.

Freezing: Layer on baking paper and seal in an airtight container. Alternatively, allow the balls to freeze on a baking tray, then pop the frozen balls into a ziplock bag. Freeze for up to 1 month.

Thawing: The balls will defrost in about 5 minutes on the kitchen counter. But they are nice cold, so pop them into your serving dish frozen – the outer balls will defrost first.

Hints & Tips

* Store in the fridge covered in plastic wrap for up to a week.
* Place balls in a small box lined with pretty paper for an amazing food gift for Christmas.

Apricot Balls

Apricot Balls are easy to make and a time-honoured tradition in my family. Enjoy!

500 g dried apricots, finely chopped

1 x 395 g can sweetened condensed milk

2½ cups shredded coconut, plus extra for rolling

Combine all the ingredients in a large bowl. Take one teaspoonful of mixture at a time and roll into a tight ball, then roll in the extra coconut. Place on a plate and refrigerate for a couple of hours before serving.

＊ ＊

Freezing: Layer on baking paper and seal in an airtight container. Alternatively, allow the balls to freeze on a baking tray then pop the frozen balls into a ziplock bag. Freeze for up to 1 month.

Thawing: The balls will defrost in about 5 minutes on the kitchen counter. But they are nice cold, so pop them into your serving dish frozen – the outer balls will defrost first.

Hints & Tips

＊ Store in the fridge in an airtight container for up to a week.

Cherry Ripe Cheesecake Balls

This Cherry Ripe Cheesecake Balls recipe is one of my family's favourites. We love Cherry Ripes and we love cheesecake – roll them together and you have a fantastic treat to eat!

250 g cream cheese, softened

1 tablespoon sugar

¾ cup shredded coconut, plus extra for coating

4 Cherry Ripe bars, diced

shaved chocolate, for coating (any flavour you like)

Beat the cream cheese and sugar with an electric mixer until smooth. Add the coconut and mix well, then add the Cherry Ripe bars and mix with a wooden spoon. Take one teaspoonful of mixture at a time and roll into a ball. Place the extra coconut and the shaved chocolate in separate small bowls, and roll the balls in the shaved chocolate and coconut to coat. Refrigerate for 1 hour before serving.

* *

Freezing: Layer on baking paper and seal in an airtight container. Alternatively, allow the balls to freeze on a baking tray then pop the frozen balls into a ziplock bag. Freeze for up to 1 month.

Thawing: The balls will defrost in about 5 minutes on the kitchen counter. But they are nice cold, so pop them into your serving dish frozen – the outer balls will defrost first.

Hints & Tips

* The balls must be stored in an airtight container in the fridge at all times unless serving. They will keep for 4–5 days.

* You can substitute chocolate dukkah for the shaved chocolate. It can be bought in specialty cake-making stores and from some supermarkets. Alternatively, you can replace it with drinking chocolate.

Chocolate Condensed Milk Balls

Chocolate Condensed Milk Balls are always popular as they are fun to make and their rich flavour is irresistible!

1 packet Marie biscuits

1 × 395 g can sweetened condensed milk

½ cup cocoa

½ cup shredded coconut, plus extra for coating

Crush the biscuits well in a food processor. Add the condensed milk, cocoa and coconut and mix together. Roll teaspoonfuls of the mixture into balls and then roll in the extra coconut and refrigerate.

Freezing: Layer on baking paper and seal in an airtight container. Alternatively, allow the balls to freeze on a baking tray then pop the frozen balls into a ziplock bag. Freeze for up to 1 month.

Thawing: The balls will defrost in about 5 minutes on the kitchen counter. But they are nice cold, so pop them into your serving dish frozen – the outer balls will defrost first.

Hints & Tips

* Store in the fridge in an airtight container for up to a week.
* You could roll the balls in chocolate sprinkles instead of coconut.

Milo Balls

Milo Balls are a great lunch box treat for the kids or a retro party food for the grown-ups. They are really easy to make and because they can be frozen, you can make them in advance!

1 packet Milk Arrowroot biscuits

3–4 tablespoons Milo

1 × 395 g can sweetened condensed milk

shredded coconut, for coating

Crush the biscuits in a food processor until fine. Add the Milo and condensed milk and mix until well combined. Take one teaspoonful of mixture at a time and roll into a ball and then roll in the shredded coconut to coat. Refrigerate for 30 minutes or until firm.

* *

Freezing: Layer on baking paper and seal in an airtight container. Alternatively, allow the balls to freeze on a baking tray then pop the frozen balls into a ziplock bag. Freeze for up to 1 month.

Thawing: The balls will defrost in about 5 minutes on the kitchen counter. But they are nice cold, so pop them into your serving dish frozen – the outer balls will defrost first.

Hints & Tips

* Store in the fridge in an airtight container for a week.
* If you are not a fan of coconut, the balls can be rolled in sifted cocoa powder or chocolate sprinkles.

Tim Tam Balls

Tim Tam Balls are a decadent combination of cream cheese mixed with any of the various flavours of Tim Tam biscuits. They freeze really well too so you can make them in advance. They make a nice change from Rum Balls (page 206).

2 packets Tim Tams (any flavour you like)

250 g cream cheese, softened

shredded coconut, for coating

In a food processor, blend the Tim Tams until fine. Add the cream cheese and process until just combined (don't over-process). Refrigerate for 30 minutes. Take one teaspoonful of mixture at a time and roll into a ball, then roll in shredded coconut.

Freezing: Layer on baking paper and seal in an airtight container. Alternatively, allow the balls to freeze on a baking tray then pop the frozen balls into a ziplock bag. Freeze for up to 1 month.

Thawing: The balls will defrost in about 5 minutes on the kitchen counter. But they are nice cold, so pop them into your serving dish frozen – the outer balls will defrost first.

Hints & Tips

* Tim Tam Balls can be served immediately or popped in the fridge to harden slightly.
* Store in the fridge in an airtight container for a week.

Cakes

Cakes not only freeze
beautifully, they defrost
perfectly too. I always keep
a cake or two in the freezer for a
morning tea or to take to a friend's
house if they aren't feeling well. As
well as cakes do freeze, icing doesn't
freeze well – so add icing later –
or just cut up and serve with
a slab of butter.

Frugal Chocolate Mud Cake

It was soooo hard to find a recipe for a chocolate mud cake without chocolate. Why do I want to do that, you say? Because chocolate is expensive! I try very hard to keep my recipes awesomely simple and cheap. Frugal Chocolate Mud Cake is certainly not as heavy as a traditional mud cake, but is heavier than a standard chocolate cake.

60 g cocoa

180 g plain flour

1 teaspoon bicarbonate of soda

125 g butter

300 g caster sugar

2 eggs

CHOCOLATE ICING

2 cups icing sugar

1½ tablespoons cocoa

1 tablespoon butter, melted

Preheat the oven to 180°C. Grease a round cake tin. Mix the cocoa with one cup of cold tap water and set aside. In another bowl, sift the flour and the bicarbonate of soda together and set aside. Beat together the butter and sugar until light and fluffy. Add the eggs one at a time, beating well with each addition. Add the cocoa mixture and the flour mixture alternately, bit by bit, until all are mixed in well. Pour into the cake tin and bake for 1 hour. Allow the cake to cool in the tin. Meanwhile, to make the chocolate icing, sift the icing sugar and cocoa together into a bowl. Pour in the melted butter and beat with a wooden spoon until smooth. Ice the cake with chocolate icing when the cake is at room temperature.

Freezing: Allow to cool to room temperature. Double wrap the un-iced cake in plastic wrap, ensuring there are no air pockets between the cake and the plastic wrap. Freeze for up to 2 months.

Thawing: Allow to sit on the kitchen counter for 20–30 minutes.

Caramel Mud Cake

*Caramel Mud Cake is a little tricky to master but it's worth it in the end.
This recipe is (I hope) easy to follow and the finished cake tastes just divine.*

185 g butter

150 g white chocolate, chopped

1 cup brown sugar

⅓ cup golden syrup

1 cup milk

1½ cups plain flour

½ cup self-raising flour

2 eggs, lightly beaten

crushed walnuts, to decorate (optional)

WHITE CHOCOLATE GANACHE

250 g white chocolate, chopped

⅓ cup thickened cream

Preheat the oven to 160°C. Grease a round cake tin and line with baking paper. Combine the butter, chocolate, sugar, syrup and milk in a saucepan over medium heat. Stir until the butter and chocolate have melted and the sugar has dissolved. Cool for 15 minutes. Whisk in the flours and eggs. Pour into the cake tin and bake for 70 minutes, covering with foil after 35 minutes to prevent over-browning. Cool for 30 minutes in the tin, then remove to a wire rack. Meanwhile, to make the ganache, combine the white chocolate and cream over a low heat, stirring until smooth. Let stand until spreadable. Spread the ganache over the cake when the cake is at room temperature. Top with crushed walnuts, if using.

* *

Freezing: Allow to cool to room temperature. Double wrap the un-iced cake in plastic wrap, ensuring there are no air pockets between the cake and the plastic wrap. Freeze for up to 2 months.

Thawing: Allow to sit on the kitchen counter for 20–30 minutes.

White Chocolate Mud Cake

White Chocolate Mud Cake is a very special cake fit for a birthday, engagement or even a wedding. Not as dense as a traditional mud cake, it is very decadent nonetheless.

250 g butter

180 g good quality white chocolate, coarsely chopped

1¼ cups caster sugar

¾ cup milk

1½ cups plain flour

½ cup self-raising flour

1 teaspoon vanilla extract

2 eggs

WHITE CHOCOLATE GANACHE

250 g white chocolate, chopped

⅓ cup thickened cream

Preheat the oven to 170°C. Grease a round cake tin and line with baking paper. Combine the butter, chocolate, sugar and milk in a medium saucepan. Stir over a low heat without boiling until smooth. Transfer the mixture to a large bowl and cool to room temperature. Sift together the flours and fold into the mixture. Add the vanilla and eggs and stir to combine. Pour into the cake tin and bake for 1½ hours, or until a skewer inserted into the centre comes out clean. Let the cake sit in the tin for 5 minutes before turning onto a wire rack to cool. Meanwhile, to make the ganache, combine the white chocolate and cream over a low heat, stirring until smooth. Let stand until spreadable. Spread the ganache over the cake when the cake is at room temperature.

Freezing: Allow to cool to room temperature. Double wrap the un-iced cake in plastic wrap, ensuring there are no air pockets between the cake and the plastic wrap. Freeze for up to 2 months.

Thawing: Allow to sit on the kitchen counter for 20–30 minutes.

Chocolate Slab Cake

Sometimes only a chocolate cake hits the spot. Feel free to top with chocolate icing for an even more chocolatey treat.

1½ cups brown sugar

150 g butter

½ teaspoon bicarbonate of soda

3 tablespoons cocoa, sifted

1½ cups self-raising flour, sifted

2 eggs

Preheat the oven to 180°C. Line a lamington tin with baking paper. In a medium saucepan, mix together the sugar, butter, bicarbonate of soda, cocoa and 1 cup of water. Heat gently over low heat until the butter is melted and the sugar is dissolved. Increase the heat and cook, stirring continuously, for 5 minutes. Bring the mixture to the boil, then reduce the heat and simmer for 2 minutes. Remove from the heat and allow to cool to room temperature. Add the flour and eggs and beat until smooth and pale. Pour into the lamington tin and bake for 30–35 minutes, or until a skewer inserted into the centre comes out clean. Turn onto a wire rack to cool.

* *

Freezing: Allow to cool to room temperature. Double wrap in plastic wrap, ensuring there are no air pockets between the cake and the plastic wrap. Freeze for up to 2 months.

Thawing: Allow to sit on the kitchen counter for 20–30 minutes.

Fruit Salad Cake

This Fruit Salad Cake recipe has only three ingredients. Plus, it is dairy-and egg-free, so all can enjoy it!

2 cups self-raising flour

1 cup sugar

1 × 440 g can fruit salad mix in syrup

Preheat the oven to 200°C. Grease a cake tin. Mix all the ingredients together until well combined. Pour into the tin and bake for 45 minutes, or until slightly brown on top.

Freezing: Allow to cool to room temperature. Double wrap in plastic wrap, ensuring there are no air pockets between the cake and the plastic wrap. Freeze for up to 2 months.

Thawing: Allow to sit on the kitchen counter for 20–30 minutes.

Hints & Tips

* If the bottom is a bit soggy, flip the cake upside down and place back in the switched-off oven for a few minutes – it will get rid of the sogginess.
* Yes, you can use fruit salad in juice instead of syrup, but it will be soggier – use the above tip to fix it.
* You can also make muffins from this recipe. Use a 12-hole muffin tin lined with paper cases, and bake at 200°C for 15–20 minutes, or until lightly golden.

Jelly Cake

This is another of my mum's recipes. You can use whatever flavour jelly you like – I love strawberry and pineapple!

125 g butter

½ cup caster sugar

2 eggs

1⅓ cups self-raising flour

½ cup milk

1 packet jelly crystals (any flavour)

2½ cups desiccated coconut

Preheat the oven to 180°C. Grease a square cake tin and line with baking paper. Using beaters, cream the butter and sugar until light and creamy. Beat in the eggs until just combined. Fold in the flour and milk until smooth. Pour the mixture into the cake tin and bake for 20–25 minutes or until a skewer inserted into the centre comes out clean. Allow to cool on a wire rack. While waiting for the cake to cool, mix the jelly crystals with 1 cup of boiling water and stir until the crystals have dissolved. Add 200 ml of cold water and chill until partially set. Cut the cake into squares, then dip in the jelly mixture and roll in the coconut. Place on a baking tray and chill for 30 minutes.

* *

Freezing: Allow to cool to room temperature. Double wrap in plastic wrap, ensuring there are no air pockets between the cake and the plastic wrap. Freeze for up to 2 months.

Thawing: Allow to sit on the kitchen counter for 20–30 minutes.

Rainbow Cupcakes

Rainbow Cupcakes look amazing! Kids love them because they not only taste incredible, but they are super eye-catching. Try them out; everyone will love making them and eating them.

½ cup caster sugar

125 g butter

2 eggs

1 cup self-raising flour

1 teaspoon vanilla extract

3 tablespoons milk

4 bottles food colouring, (red, blue, yellow, green)

Hints & Tips

* For brighter colours, add half a teaspoon of white vinegar to every bowl.

Preheat the oven to 200°C. Line a 12-hole cupcake tin with paper cases. Cream the sugar and butter together until light and fluffy. Beat the eggs in one at a time, adding a little of the flour each time until the ingredients are mixed. Add the vanilla and mix well, then add the milk 1 tablespoon at a time, mixing after each addition. Divide the mixture into six bowls:

* In bowl 1, add half a cap of blue and half a cap of red food colouring
* In bowl 2, add half a cap of blue
* In bowl 3, add half a cap of green
* In bowl 4, add half a cap of yellow
* In bowl 5, add half a cap of red and half a cap of yellow
* In bowl 6, add half a cap of red

Mix the food colouring into the cake mixture. Divide the mixture in bowl 1 between the 12 muffin cases. Repeat with the other mixtures in order. Bake for 10–15 minutes, or until a skewer inserted into the centre comes out clean.

*   *
  *

Freezing: Allow to cool to room temperature. Double wrap in plastic wrap, ensuring there are no air pockets between the cakes and the plastic wrap. Freeze for up to 2 months.

Thawing: Allow to sit on the kitchen counter for 20–30 minutes.

Mixed Berry and
White Chocolate Muffins

*Our Mixed Berry and White Chocolate Muffins recipe is not the most frugal –
but it is nice for a special occasion like a birthday or Christmas Day!*

2 cups plain flour

3 teaspoons baking
powder

¾ cup caster sugar

½ cup shredded
coconut

1 cup white chocolate
chips (finely chopped
or crushed)

1 cup milk

2 eggs

1 teaspoon vanilla
extract

100 g butter, melted
and cooled slightly

1 cup frozen mixed
berries

icing sugar, for dusting
(optional)

Preheat the oven to 180°C. Grease a 12-hole
muffin tin or line with muffin cases. Sift the flour
and baking powder together into a large bowl.
Stir in the caster sugar, coconut and chocolate.
In a large jug, whisk together the milk, eggs,
vanilla and butter until well combined. Slowly
pour into the dry mixture, stirring with a metal
spoon, until just combined. Gently swirl the
frozen mixed berries through (do not over-mix).
Spoon the mixture into the muffin tin. Bake for
25–30 minutes, or until a skewer inserted into the
centre comes out clean. Allow to stand in the tin
for 5 minutes before turning out onto a wire rack
to cool. Lightly dust with icing sugar, if desired.

* *

Freezing: Allow to cool to room temperature.
Double wrap in plastic wrap, ensuring there are
no air pockets between the muffins and the plastic
wrap. Freeze for up to 2 months.

Thawing: Allow to sit on the kitchen counter for
20–30 minutes.

Sultana Butter Cake

Remember having a slab of Sultana Butter Cake with butter on top at Nan's house? Make a double or triple batch of this cake and freeze some for when unexpected visitors arrive.

3 black tea bags

1 cup boiling water

2 cups sultanas

125 g butter

¾ cup caster sugar

2 eggs, beaten

1 teaspoon vanilla extract

¾ cup self-raising flour

¾ cup plain flour

¼ cup milk

Place the tea bags in a medium bowl and pour the boiling water over the top. Leave to stand for a few minutes. Remove the teabags and add the sultanas to the tea and let them 'steep' for 20 minutes. Pour off any excess liquid and discard. Preheat the oven to 180°C and grease a loaf tin. Beat the butter and sugar together until creamed. Add the beaten eggs and vanilla and stir to combine. In a separate bowl sift the flours together. Add the egg mixture to the sultana mixture, alternately with the sifted flours and milk and fold to combine. Pour into the loaf tin and bake for 60 minutes, or until a skewer inserted into the centre comes out clean. Transfer to a wire rack to cool. Serve warm with butter.

Freezing: Allow to cool to room temperature. Double wrap in plastic wrap, ensuring there are no air pockets between the cake and the plastic wrap. Freeze for up to 2 months.

Thawing: Allow to sit on the kitchen counter for 20–30 minutes.

Banana Loaf

Banana Loaf is a deliciously sweet and easy treat to make. It is suitable for freezing and a slice makes for a great snack at morning tea time.

1 cup plain flour

½ cup self-raising flour

1 cup brown sugar

1 teaspoon cinnamon

2 eggs, whisked

125 g butter, melted then cooled

3 or 4 ripe bananas, mashed

½ cup sultanas (optional)

Preheat the oven to 180°C. Grease and line a loaf tin. Sift the flours, sugar and cinnamon into a large mixing bowl. In a separate bowl, whisk the eggs and butter together then add to the dry mixture. Stir in the mashed banana and sultanas, if using. Mix until just combined. Spoon the mixture into the loaf tin and smooth the surface. Bake for 45–50 minutes, or until a skewer inserted into the centre comes out clean. Set aside in the pan to cool for 10 minutes before turning out onto a wire rack. Serve warm, spread with butter.

Freezing: Allow to cool to room temperature. Double wrap in plastic wrap, ensuring there are no air pockets between the cake and the plastic wrap. Freeze for up to 2 months.

Thawing: Allow to sit on the kitchen counter for 20–30 minutes.

Hints & Tips

* For an even more 'evil' version, add half a cup of chocolate chips.
* If you have bananas in your fruit bowl that are starting to turn black, don't throw them out! Remove the skin and place in a ziplock bag. They freeze well for 2 months.

Catering to Allergies

Here are some recipes that allow for the fact that someone in your family may have a food intolerance, which is becoming more and more common.

Banana Ice-cream

Banana Ice-Cream is a low-fat, dairy-free dessert that you can make in about one minute flat. This is a great way to use overripe bananas. If you have some in your fruit bowl, just peel them, place in a ziplock bag and pop in the freezer. Then you can make this ice-cream whenever you like!

1 frozen banana
per person

Add the frozen bananas to a food processor and whip until the consistency of soft serve ice-cream. Serve piled high in a bowl!

Freezing: Place into a shallow sealed container and freeze for up to 1 month.

Thawing: Not suitable for thawing. Eat frozen.

Dairy-free Strawberry Ice-cream

Want a dairy-free, egg-free and sugar-free strawberry ice-cream? Well try this one – it tastes fantastic. Very refreshing and super easy, especially if you have an ice-cream maker on hand. It's almost gelato-like.

250 g strawberries

1 × 400 ml can coconut milk

1 teaspoon vanilla extract

2 teaspoons sugar replacement sweetener (or 2 tablespoons honey)

pinch of salt

Wash the strawberries well and cut off the tops. Place in a food processor and process until they aren't quite liquid. Pour into a jug and stir in the coconut milk, vanilla extract, sweetener and salt, mixing well. Pour into an ice-cream maker and mix for 50 minutes.

* *

Freezing: Place into a shallow sealed container and freeze for up to 1 month.

Thawing: Not suitable for thawing. Eat frozen.

Hints & Tips

* If you don't have an ice-cream maker, just freeze the mixture for 45 minutes, then take out of the freezer and use electric beaters to beat it for 3 minutes. Then freeze overnight.

Dairy-free Chocolate Coconut Cake

Everyone loves chocolate cake, and now you can enjoy it even if you have a dairy intolerance.

380 g dairy-free dark chocolate, chopped

2 × 400 ml cans coconut milk

1 cup brown sugar

2¼ cups self-raising flour, sifted

1 teaspoon baking powder

1 teaspoon vanilla extract

Preheat the oven to 180°C. Line a round cake tin with baking paper. Half fill a medium saucepan with water and place over medium heat. Place a metal bowl on top of the saucepan (the water should not touch the base of the bowl). Add half the chocolate and half the coconut milk to the bowl and stir until the mixture is melted and smooth. Remove from the heat. Add the sugar, flour, baking powder and vanilla extract to the chocolate mixture and beat for a couple of minutes, or until well combined. Pour into the cake tin and bake for 35 minutes or until a skewer inserted into the centre comes out clean. Turn onto a wire rack to cool. Heat the remaining chocolate and coconut milk in the metal bowl over the saucepan and stir until smooth. Pour the chocolate sauce over the cooled cake and serve.

Freezing: Allow to cool to room temperature. Double wrap the un-sauced cake in plastic wrap. Freeze for up to 6 months.

Thawing: Allow to sit on the kitchen counter for 10–15 minutes.

Hints & Tips

* Dairy-free chocolate is available from healthfood stores and some supermarkets.

Dairy- and Egg-free Cake

This cake is perfect to take to school or day care as a surprise. It is moist and delicious and will be a winner for kids with food allergies!

1½ cups self-raising flour

1 cup caster sugar

¼ cup cocoa

½ teaspoon salt

⅓ cup vegetable oil

1 teaspoon vanilla extract

1 teaspoon white vinegar

DAIRY-FREE VIENNA ICING

125 g Nuttelex

1½ cups icing sugar

2 tablespoons rice milk or water

Preheat the oven to 150°C. Line a round cake tin with baking paper. Sift the flour, sugar, cocoa and salt together into a bowl. Add the oil, vanilla extract, white vinegar and 1 cup of water. Mix with hand beaters on high until smooth. Pour into the cake tin and bake for 40–45 minutes, until a skewer inserted into the centre comes out clean. Allow to cool. Meanwhile, to make the icing, beat the Nuttelex until as white as possible. Gradually add half the icing sugar, beating continuously. Add the milk or water then the remaining icing sugar. Spread over the cake when the cake is at room temperature.

* *

Freezing: Allow to cool to room temperature. Double wrap the un-iced cake in plastic wrap. Freeze for up to 1 month.

Thawing: Allow to sit on the kitchen counter for 10–15 minutes.

Hints & Tips

* Dairy- and Egg-free Cake can be doubled and cooked in slab tins for birthday cakes.
* To make a vanilla version, omit the cocoa and add a little extra vanilla extract if you like.
* Can be made as cupcakes. Place in a 12-hole muffin tin lined with paper cases and bake for 10 minutes at 150°C.

Dairy- and Egg-free Pancakes

These pancakes taste exactly the same as ordinary pancakes; the only difference is that everyone can eat these!

1 cup plain flour

½ teaspoon bicarbonate of soda

2 teaspoons baking powder

¼ teaspoon salt

2 tablespoons sugar

1½ tablespoons vegetable oil

½ teaspoon vanilla essence

1 cup soymilk (or water)

cooking oil spray

Sift the flour, bicarbonate of soda, baking powder and salt together into a bowl. Add the sugar and mix well. Add the oil, vanilla and half the soymilk and whisk until well combined. Slowly add the rest of the soymilk, whisking continuously, until the mixture is of a thick pouring consistency. Heat a frying pan over medium heat and spray with cooking oil. Pour in enough mixture in to make a pancake, swirling the mixture to cover the base of the pan. Cook until bubbles appear on the top of the pancake, flip and cook for a further minute.

* *

Freezing: Allow to cool then stack between sheets of baking paper and place in a sealed airtight container. Freeze for up to 1 week.

Thawing: Allow to sit on the kitchen counter for 5 minutes.

Reheating: Either microwave the pancakes until warm, or pop them in the toaster – easy and efficient way to heat them!

Hints & Tips

* Serve with lemon and sugar or bacon and maple syrup!
* You can also use this recipe to make pikelets rather than pancakes.

Gluten-free White Chocolate Cake

This white chocolate cake was so yum when I first made it that it barely lasted the day!

250 g white chocolate, chopped

½ cup butter

¼ cup caster sugar

5 eggs, separated

¾ cup almond meal

icing sugar, for sprinkling

Preheat the oven to 180°C. Line a round cake tin with baking paper. In a saucepan over low heat, combine the white chocolate, butter and caster sugar. Stir until the chocolate and butter are melted and the sugar dissolved. Remove from the heat and allow to cool for a few minutes, but don't let it set. Add the egg yolks one at a time, stirring after each addition. Add the almond meal and mix until well combined. Whisk the egg whites until stiff then fold gently into the almond mixture. Pour into the cake tin and bake for 50 minutes, until lightly brown and the centre springs back when gently pressed. Cover with foil if the top browns too quickly. Cool for 5 minutes in the tin then turn onto a wire rack to cool completely. Dust with icing sugar.

Freezing: Allow to cool to room temperature then double wrap in plastic wrap. Freeze for up to 1 month.

Thawing: Allow to sit on the kitchen counter for 10–15 minutes.

Gluten-free Almond and Raspberry Cake

This recipe makes a nice change from the traditional almond and orange combination. Almond meal is delicious in cakes and this one is no exception!

PASTRY

1 cup rice flour

²⁄₃ cup cornflour

½ cup buckwheat flour

200 g butter

2 eggs

CAKE

1½ cups frozen raspberries

¾ cup caster sugar

125 g butter

⅓ cup caster sugar

3 eggs

¾ cup almond meal

½ cup cornflour

Hints & Tips

* The pastry can also be made in a food processor by pulsing the flours and butter until they resemble breadcrumbs then adding one egg at a time and processing until combined.

Preheat the oven to 180°C. Grease and line a flan dish. To make the pastry, mix the rice flour, cornflour and buckwheat flour together in a large bowl. Mix in the butter with your fingertips until the mixture resembles breadcrumbs. Add the eggs one at a time, mixing well after each addition with electric beaters. Press into the flan dish. Bake for 15 minutes, or until lightly golden. Remove and allow to cool slightly. Meanwhile, to make the cake, combine the raspberries and sugar in a saucepan over medium heat. Stir until the sugar dissolves and the mixture comes to the boil. Simmer for 8–10 minutes, or until the mixture thickens. Remove from the heat and allow to cool. Cream the butter and sugar together in a large bowl, then add the eggs one at a time, beating well after each addition. Stir in the almond meal and cornflour until well combined. Spread the cooled raspberry mixture over the pastry base then top with the almond mixture, using a knife to smooth it. Bake for 30 minutes, or until golden.

Freezing: Layer slices of the cake between sheets of baking paper and seal in an airtight container. Freeze for up to 2 weeks.

Thawing: Allow to sit on the kitchen counter for 30 minutes. The cake must be eaten within 12 hours or it will become soft.

Gluten-free Banana Bread

A delicious slice of toasted banana bread, served piping hot with a cup of tea, is a true delight. But as many people are sensitive to gluten, I didn't want our coeliac sisters to miss out. This gluten-free version is just as delectable as the real thing!

125 g Nuttelex

¾ cup caster sugar

2 eggs

2 medium over-ripe bananas

¾ cup gluten-free self-raising flour

¼ cup rice flour

½ cup gluten-free plain flour

½ teaspoon bicarbonate of soda

Preheat the oven to 180°C. Grease a loaf pan and line with baking paper. Place the Nuttelex and caster sugar into a bowl and beat with an electric mixer until light and creamy. Add the eggs one at a time, stirring after each addition, and combine well. Mash the bananas with a fork, add to the mixture and use a wooden spoon to combine. Sift the flours and bicarbonate of soda together then fold gently into the mixture. Pour into the loaf tin and bake for 55 minutes, or until a skewer inserted into the centre comes out clean. Cool in the tin for 10 minutes before tipping onto a wire rack to cool completely.

Freezing: Allow to cool to room temperature then double wrap in plastic wrap. Freeze for up to 2 months.

Thawing: Allow to sit on the kitchen counter for 10–15 minutes.

Hints & Tips

* Gluten-free Banana Bread is best eaten fresh on the day it is made.

Christmas Fare

Ahhhh, Christmas –
my favourite time of year!
As I'm usually the one cooking
in the kitchen (because I love it and
because I'm a mum and like most of us get
stuck with the job ...) I like to make my life
as easy as possible during the festive season so
I can sit back and enjoy a few beverages on the
big day. Because Christmas is always so darn
hot, it makes sense to have cold desserts and
snacks – and all these can be made in
advance and frozen so you just have
to pop them out of the freezer
before serving.

Rum Balls

Rum Balls are a traditional favourite loved by generations of people. You don't have to just make them at Christmas time; they are good all year round. They also make a great present for a boss, co-worker, teacher — well, anyone really!

1 cup chopped raisins or sultanas

2 tablespoons rum (or more depending on taste!)

8 Weetbix, crushed

2 tablespoons cocoa

½ cup shredded coconut, plus extra for coating

1 × 395 g can sweetened condensed milk

Place the raisins or sultanas and the rum in a metal bowl, cover with plastic wrap and leave to marinate for a day. Place the crushed Weetbix, cocoa, coconut and marinated fruit into a bowl, pour over the condensed milk and stir well. Roll teaspoonfuls of the mixture into balls and roll in the coconut. Place on a plate and chill in the fridge for 30 minutes to firm up before serving.

Freezing: Layer on baking paper and seal in an airtight container. Alternatively, allow the balls to freeze on a baking tray then pop the frozen balls into a ziplock bag. Freeze for up to 1 month.

Thawing: The balls will defrost in about 5 minutes on the kitchen counter. But they are nice cold, so pop them into your serving dish frozen — the outer balls will defrost first.

North Pole Balls

Yes, we managed to find some more yummy balls just in time for Christmas. These will not disappoint!

2 packets white chocolate Tim Tams

250 g cream cheese, softened

¾ cup shredded coconut

36 candy canes

⅓ cup white chocolate, melted

36 red M&M's (you can sometimes buy Christmas M&M's that only have red and green)

Place the Tim Tams into a food processor and chop into chunks. Add the cream cheese and blend until just combined (1–2 minutes). Roll heaped teaspoonfuls of the mixture into balls then roll in the coconut. Refrigerate for 30 minutes to firm up before decorating. Cut the curved ends off the candy canes so they are sticks. Place a ball on one end of a candy cane. Top the ball with a quarter teaspoon of melted white chocolate and place an M&M on top. Repeat for the remaining balls.

Freezing: Layer on baking paper and seal in an airtight container. Alternatively, allow the balls to freeze on a baking tray then pop the frozen balls into a ziplock bag. Freeze for up to 1 month.

Thawing: The balls will defrost in about 5 minutes on the kitchen counter. But they are nice cold, so pop them into your serving dish frozen – the outer balls will defrost first.

White Christmas Crackles

Chocolate crackles are all the rage for kids' birthday parties, but what about adapting the recipe to suit Christmas? Enter these delicious White Christmas Crackles – so easy the kids can make them!

3 cups Rice Bubbles

1 cup shredded coconut

¾ cup icing sugar, sifted

1 cup powdered milk

1 cup mixed dried fruit

250 g copha

50 g glacé cherries, chopped

Combine all the dry ingredients except the cherries in a mixing bowl. Melt the copha slowly over a low heat, cool slightly and pour onto the dry ingredients. Mix well then fold the glacé cherries through. Spoon the mixture into paper cases and freeze for 30 minutes until set.

* *

Freezing: Layer on baking paper and seal in an airtight container. Alternatively, allow the crackles to freeze on a baking tray then place into a ziplock bag. Freeze for up to 2 weeks.

Thawing: The crackles will defrost in about 5 minutes on the kitchen counter. But they are nice cold, so pop them into your serving dish frozen – the outer crackles will defrost first.

Hints & Tips

* White Christmas Crackles should be kept in an airtight container for up to 5 days.

Mini Mars Bar Christmas Puddings

Mini Mars Bar Christmas Puddings contain everything kids love. Chocolate, Rice Bubbles . . . and more chocolate! It's a novel idea for a Christmas dessert.

canola oil spray

200 g Mars Bars, chopped

2 tablespoons pouring cream

2 teaspoons cocoa, sifted

3 cups Rice Bubbles

100 g white chocolate

24 Christmas M&M's

Spray the holes in two 12-hole mini-muffin tins with canola oil. Melt the Mars Bar, cream and cocoa together in a glass bowl placed over a saucepan of simmering water. (The bowl should not touch the water.) Stir the mixture until smooth. Put the Rice Bubbles in a separate bowl, pour in the chocolate mixture and stir until well combined. Spoon the mixture into the muffin tins and press down gently. Refrigerate for 2 hours then turn out onto a tray to decorate. Melt the white chocolate and add 1 teaspoon to each pudding then top with an M&M.

* *

Freezing: Layer on baking paper and seal in an airtight container. Alternatively, allow the puddings to freeze on a baking tray, then pop the into a ziplock bag. Freeze for up to 3 weeks.

Thawing: Allow to sit on the kitchen counter for 5 minutes.

Frozen Christmas Pudding

This is a good alternative pudding for our usual hot Australian Christmas Days. It looks classy and tastes divine!

CUSTARD

2 cups vanilla custard

320 ml double cream

½ cup caster sugar

1 teaspoon vanilla bean paste

CHOCOLATE CUSTARD CENTRE

2½ cups chocolate custard

2½ cups vanilla ice-cream

160 ml thickened cream

1½ cups diced fruitcake

½ cup mixed nuts (we used cashews, almonds and peanuts)

Mix all the custard ingredients together in an ice-cream maker according to the maker's instructions, until thick and just set. (If you don't have an ice-cream maker you can mix all the ingredients together in a bowl then place in the freezer for 1 hour until just set.) Grease a pudding tin with butter and line with plastic wrap, allowing some overhang. Spread the semifrozen custard around the base and sides to evenly coat the tin. Freeze for 1 hour while you prepare the chocolate custard centre. Mix the chocolate custard, vanilla ice-cream and cream together in an ice-cream maker until thick and just set. (Again, if you don't have an ice-cream maker you can mix all the ingredients together in a bowl then place in the freezer for 1 hour until just set.) Fold in the fruitcake and nuts, pour into the pudding tin, cover with plastic wrap and place in the freezer for 4 hours or overnight. To remove the pudding, invert the tin onto a chopping board and place a hot tea towel around the tin for a minute. Turn upright and, holding the pudding tin firm, pull the plastic wrap up. Invert onto a serving plate and peel off the plastic wrap.

Hints & Tips

* One way I like to decorate the frozen pudding is by pouring melted chocolate over the top and then adding raspberries and mint leaves.

Freezing: Freeze for up to 3 months.

Thawing: Do not thaw; eat from frozen.

Fruit Mince Truffles

Fruit Mince Truffles are so very yummy. Dark chocolate is an antioxidant, nuts have your protein, butter is your dairy and fruit mince is your fruit – so really this is a healthy snack!

375 g dark chocolate, chopped

80 g butter, chopped

1 cup fruit mince

½ cup chopped almonds

cocoa or chocolate sprinkles, for coating

Melt the chocolate in a glass bowl over a saucepan of simmering water and stir until smooth. Remove from the heat and add the butter, one piece at a time, stirring until well combined and smooth. Add the fruit mince and almonds, and combine well. Cover and refrigerate for 1 hour or until firm. Roll tablespoonfuls into balls and coat with cocoa or sprinkles. Refrigerate until ready to serve.

Freezing: Layer on baking paper and seal in an airtight container. Alternatively, allow the truffles to freeze on a baking tray then place into a ziplock bag. Freeze for up to 2 weeks.

Thawing: The truffles will defrost in about 5 minutes on the kitchen counter. But they are nice cold, so pop them into your serving dish frozen – the outer truffles will defrost first.

Fruit Mince Cheesecakes

Fruit Mince Cheesecakes make for an easy cold dessert for Christmas Day. They only contain dried fruit, not fruit mince, so you don't have to go and buy fruit mince specially!

250 g gingernut biscuits

80 g butter, melted

1 cup dried fruit and nuts

250 g cream cheese, softened

⅓ cup white chocolate buttons, melted

¼ cup caster sugar

200 g sour cream

2 eggs

icing sugar, to decorate

Preheat the oven to 160°C. Line two 12-hole muffin tins with foil pushed into each hole. In a food processor, process the biscuits until they resemble breadcrumbs. Add the melted butter. Process to combine then divide the mixture between the holes in the muffin tin. Refrigerate for 20 minutes or until firm. Process the dried fruit and nuts for 1 minute or until they resemble breadcrumbs. Using electric beaters, beat the cream cheese, melted white chocolate and sugar together until smooth. Add the sour cream, eggs and the fruit and nut mixture. Mix thoroughly then spoon on top of the biscuit bases. Bake for 20–25 minutes, or until firm. Turn off the oven, open the door slightly and allow the cheesecakes to cool in the oven. Refrigerate overnight. Dust with icing sugar to serve.

Freezing: Layer on baking paper and seal in an airtight container. Freeze for up to 2 weeks.

Thawing: Allow to sit on the kitchen counter for 5 minutes.

Candy Cane Cookies

These didn't last long in our house last Christmas and were a massive hit as gifts to grandparents from the kids.

10 mini candy canes

125 g butter

⅔ cup brown sugar

1 teaspoon vanilla essence

1 egg

¾ cup plain flour

2 teaspoons cocoa

½ cup desiccated coconut

Preheat the oven to 150°C. Line a baking tray with baking paper. Place the candy canes in a ziplock bag and hit with a rolling pin to break them up into small pieces. Beat the butter, sugar and vanilla together until light and fluffy. Add the egg and beat again. Mix in the flour, cocoa and coconut with a flat-bladed knife, then mix in two-thirds of the crushed candy canes. Refrigerate the mix for 30 minutes, or until firm. Roll tablespoonfuls of the mixture into balls. Place on the baking tray, leaving room for the cookies to spread (use more than one tray if necessary). Press down gently to flatten slightly. Bake for 15 minutes. As soon as the cookies come out of the oven press the remaining candy cane pieces into the tops. Leave on the tray for 5 minutes then turn onto a wire rack to cool completely.

Freezing: Layer on baking paper and seal in an airtight container. Alternatively, allow the cookies to freeze on a baking tray then place into a ziplock bag. Freeze for up to 1 month.

Thawing: Allow to sit on the kitchen counter for 5 minutes.

Technical Stuff

Freezing Times and Methods for Some Common Foods

FOOD	FREEZING TIME	METHOD
Biscuits	Up to 3 months	Unbaked biscuit dough can be shaped and then frozen, or frozen in a log or balls. Wrap well. Allow to thaw in the fridge overnight.
Bread	Up to 1 month	If you have baked your own bread, cool completely before freezing in a ziplock bag. Simply defrost at room temperature for 2–3 hours.
Butter	Up to 9 months	Freeze in its original packaging, placed in a freezer bag. Thaw in the fridge overnight to prevent separation.
Cake	Iced – up to 3 months Un-iced – up to 6 months	If baking your own cake, cool completely before freezing. Place in a solid container to avoid crushing. Buttercream icing freezes well, but custards and egg whites (meringue) do not. Place the unwrapped, frosted cake in the freezer to harden the icing before wrapping. Thaw wrapped (iced in fridge, un-iced at room temperature) for 2–4 hours.
Casseroles	Up to 3 months	It's a good idea to slightly undercook the casserole so it can finish cooking when it is defrosted and reheated. Sauces with cornflour can be frozen, but for the best consistency, add the cornflour when reheating.

FOOD	FREEZING TIME	METHOD
Cheese	Up to 6 months	You cannot freeze an entire block of cheese, so grate it (either in a food processor or by hand), and freeze in ziplock bags, allowing enough room that the cheese does not clump together.
Chicken	Whole chicken – up to 3 months Chicken pieces – up to 12 months	If you have a whole chicken, rinse and pat dry then store in a ziplock bag or tightly sealed in plastic wrap with as much air squeezed out as possible. With chicken pieces, store boned pieces separately from fillets in ziplock bags. Do not re-freeze defrosted chicken.
Eggs	Uncooked – up to 6 months Cooked – not recommended In shells – not recommended	To freeze yolks separately, add a teaspoon of sugar or salt per egg yolk (depending on whether you are using them for a sweet or savoury dish). Make sure you label which one you use. Cooked items containing eggs can usually be frozen, but whole, uncooked eggs cannot.
Flour, uncooked rice, sugar, nuts and cooking chocolate	Indefinitely	Flour stored in a ziplock bag in the freezer will last twice as long as in the pantry, and it also keeps out weevils and pantry moths. Freeze sugar, nuts, cooking chocolate and rice in the summer to prevent them going stale. Just seal them tightly to avoid freezer smell.

FOOD	FREEZING TIME	METHOD
Fish	Fatty fish, such as herring, mackerel and sardines – not recommended Medium fatty fish, such as salmon and trout – up to 3 months Other fish – up to 6 months	When freezing fish, it's important to pop it in the freezer at its freshest. Vacuum sealing is preferred for freezing fish, but wrapping tightly in plastic wrap will do the job, just as long as there is no air getting to the fish. Thaw very gently.
Fruit	Not recommended for most fruit Suitable fruit – up to 6 months	Most fruits cannot be frozen due to their high water content, unless you are planning on using them frozen. Melons, apples, grapes and citrus fruits do very poorly when frozen and then thawed. Citrus zest can be grated or left whole and frozen. Freeze small fruits in a single layer on a tray until firm and then store in an airtight container.
Herbs	Sprigs – not recommended Processed – up to 3 months	Fresh soft and leafy herbs like basil, parsley and chives don't hold up well in the freezer. But you can process them into a paste, adding olive oil to prevent them from going brown and to enhance the flavour. Freeze in an ice cube container
Meat, sausages and mince	Up to 12 months	Discard any foam trays and plastic wrapping, as supermarket packaging isn't moisture-resistant and is usually quite thin; meat frozen in supermarket meat trays develops freezer burn quickly. Wrap in plastic wrap or place in a ziplock bag.

FOOD	FREEZING TIME	METHOD
Milk	Up to 3 months	Milk freezes beautifully, it just needs a bit of room for expansion. Place an almost-full plastic bottle straight into the freezer, before its use-by date, and don't be concerned when it goes yellow; it will return to white when defrosted. To defrost, simply place in the fridge for a day or two and give a good shake when you can no longer feel any solid ice inside.
Onion	Up to 12 months	A rancid onion has no place in your pantry. Grab a big bag on special, peel the skin, chop the top and tail off and cut in half. You can grate some halves, dice them finely or leave them whole and freeze in small bags. They retain their flavour but are soft on defrosting so are not suitable for salads or to be consumed raw.
Pasta	Up to 2 months	Cooked pasta loses its flavour and form when frozen; it usually becomes soggy and somewhat gluggy. So undercook it and freeze in a sauce for best results. Thaw overnight in the fridge before reheating to complete the cooking.

FOOD	FREEZING TIME	METHOD
Pastry	Unbaked – up to 3 months Baked – up to 3 months	Uncooked pastry should be rolled out into the desired shape (e.g. pie base, flat square for cutting out shapes) and then frozen, to allow for easier handling when defrosted. Separate layers of pastry with plastic wrap or baking paper and wrap tightly in plastic wrap or foil.
Sandwiches	Up to 2 weeks	Only some fillings can be frozen (see page 19). Freeze in plastic wrap or ziplock bags.
Sauces	Up to 3 months	Sauces tend to separate unless mixed with other ingredients. Sauces thickened with flour and thickeners tend not to freeze well. Homemade gravies and sauces can freeze well if put in containers that allow expansion.
Soup	Up to 6 months	Cool completely and skim any fat off the top. Place in ziplock bags, leaving room for expansion.
Tomato paste	Up to 4 months	Fill an oiled ice cube container with leftover tomato paste. The paste does not freeze solid, but once it is semi-frozen, pop into a ziplock bag and seal.

FOOD	FREEZING TIME	METHOD
Vegetables	Not recommended for most vegetables Suitable vegetables – up to 6 months	Vegetables with high water content don't freeze well and once defrosted these vegies are mushy, limp and generally unappetising. These include lettuce, sprouts, cucumbers, celery, onions, radishes, tomatoes and capsicums. Vegetables such as peas, corn, carrots, cauliflower and broccoli that are snap frozen have just as high nutritional content as fresh. Blanch vegetables before freezing for a better result (see page 20).
Wine	Up to 3 months	Leftover wine – what's that? If you've not managed to get through the bottle, freeze the leftovers in an ice cube container to add to casseroles or risottos. Be aware though that the higher the alcohol content, the more difficult it will be to freeze the wine solid.

Oven Temperature

°C	°F	GAS	METHOD
120	250	½	Very Slow
140	275	1	
150	300	2	Slow
170	325	3	
180	350	4	Moderate
190	375	5	
200	400	6	Moderately Hot
220	425	7	
230	450	8	Hot
240	475	9	Very Hot

Cooking Times

OVEN OR STOVETOP	LOW SLOW COOKER SETTING	HIGH SLOW COOKER SETTING
15–30 minutes	4–6 hours	1½–2½ hours
35–40 minutes	6–8 hours	3–4 hours
50 minutes–3 hours	8–10 hours	4–6 hours

Cup and Spoon Liquids Conversion

CUP/SPOON	MILLILITRES
1 cup	250 ml
¾ cup	180 ml
⅔ cup	160 ml
½ cup	125 ml
⅓ cup	80 ml
¼ cup	60 ml
1 tablespoon	20 ml
1 teaspoon	5 ml

Metric/Imperial Volume Conversion

METRIC VOLUME	IMPERIAL VOLUME (APPROX.)
1 litre	35 fl oz
750 ml	27 fl oz
500 ml	18 fl oz
375 ml	13 fl oz
250 ml	9 fl oz
180 ml	6 fl oz
160 ml	5½ fl oz
125 ml	4½ fl oz
80 ml	3 fl oz
60 ml	2 fl oz
20 ml	½ fl oz

Metric/Imperial Weight Conversion

METRIC WEIGHT	IMPERIAL WEIGHT (APPROX.)
1 kg	2 lb
750 g	1²/₃ lb
500 g	1 lb
375 g	13 oz
250 g	9 oz
175 g	6 oz
150 g	5 oz
100 g	3½ oz
80 g	3 oz
50 g	2 oz
10 g	¹/₃ oz

Don't forget there's more technical stuff – like seasonality tables, sample shopping lists and budgeting tools – on our website:

stayathomemum.com.au

Acknowledgements

I would like to thank Clancy Briggs, my co-writer, who helped me get this book together even though she was dealing with four kids, one of whom was a newborn. How you did it, I'll never know, but you have my eternal thanks – you are a truly talented writer and friend.

I would also like to thank my fellow Stay at Home Mum directors, Nicole Millard and Chris Gryg, for letting me off my 'work duties' to fulfil my dream of writing a book. And for never thinking I'm bonkers, when I usually am.

To Kate – my bff, neighbour and personal assistant – you make my life so easy. Thanks for putting up with me when my head is in the clouds.

I would like to thank Lydia, my food editor, for editing all my recipes and making sure they tasted as good as they possibly could.

Finally, I would like to thank my family – Brendan and the boys, Mum & Dad – and all my friends, who have supported me and had faith that I could pull this off. Thanks for being there.

Index